With
Jake.
nephew ever

Love
Auntie Carol

D0457406

How High Can You Bounce?

TURN YOUR SETBACKS INTO COMEBACKS

Roger Crawford

BANTAM BOOKS

NEW YORK • TORONTO • LONDON • SYDNEY • AUCKLAND

HOW HIGH CAN YOU BOUNCE?
A Bantam Book / January 1998

All rights reserved.
Copyright © 1998 by Roger Crawford.
BOOK DESIGN BY JESSICA SHATAN.

No part of this book may be reproduced or transmitted in any form or by any means, electronic or mechanical, including photocopying, recording, or by any information storage and retrieval system, without permission in writing from the publisher. For information address: Bantam Books.

Library of Congress Cataloging-in-Publication Data
Crawford, Roger, 1960–
How high can you bounce? : turn your setbacks into comebacks /
Roger Crawford.
p.   cm.
Includes bibliographical references.
ISBN 0-553-10461-6
1. Success—Psychological aspects.   2. Resilience (Personality trait)   I. Title.
BF637.S8C73   1998
158.1—dc21   97-36689
CIP

Published simultaneously in the United States and Canada

Bantam Books are published by Bantam Books, a division of Bantam Doubleday Dell Publishing Group, Inc. Its trademark, consisting of the words "Bantam Books" and the portrayal of a rooster, is Registered in U.S. Patent and Trademark Office and in other countries. Marca Registrada. Bantam Books, 1540 Broadway, New York, New York 10036.

PRINTED IN THE UNITED STATES OF AMERICA

BVG   10   9   8   7   6   5   4   3   2   1

MORE PRAISE FOR
HOW HIGH CAN YOU BOUNCE?

"The one quality that will guarantee you great success in life is personal resilience. In this fast-moving, practical, helpful, and inspiring book, Roger Crawford leads you step-by-step toward the development of deep reserves of that resilience and persistence that makes your success inevitable."

—Brian Tracy, author of
Maximum Achievement

"Roger has captured the essence of that most elusive and essential quality of life, human resilience. Even more remarkable, he proves that resilience can be learned."

—Alan Loy McGinnis, author of
The Power of Optimism and
The Friendship Factor

"*How High Can You Bounce?* offers a clear blueprint for harnessing your personal strength to meet those everyday challenges most effectively. Roger's experiences are a testament to the power of resilience, and he shares them with wit and loads of practical advice. I highly recommend it!"

—Tony Alessandra, Ph.D., author of
The Platinum Rule

"Roger's remarkable life story inspires us all to rise above our self-imposed limitations. Read *How High Can You Bounce?* and be elevated!"

—Michael LeBoeuf, Ph.D.,
author of *How to Win Customers and Keep Them for Life*

"The one quality that will guarantee y
personal resilience. In this fast-moving,
spiring book, Roger Crawford leads you
development of deep reserves of that i
that makes your success inevitable."

—Brian Tracy, autl
Maximum Achieve

"Roger has captured the essence of that
quality of life, human resilience. Even n
that resilience can be learned."

—Alan Loy McGinnis
The Power of Optim
The Friendship F

"*How High Can You Bounce?* offers a cl
your personal strength to meet those e
fectively. Roger's experiences are a te
silience, and he shares them with wit a
I highly recommend it!"

—Tony Alessandra, Ph
The Platinum

"Roger's remarkable life story inspires
imposed limitations. Read *How Hig*
elevated!"

—Michael LeBoeι
author of *How to Win Customers*

How High Can You Bounce?

TURN YOUR SETBACKS INTO COMEBACKS

Roger Crawford

BANTAM BOOKS

NEW YORK • TORONTO • LONDON • SYDNEY • AUCKLAND

HOW HIGH CAN YOU BOUNCE?
A Bantam Book / January 1998

All rights reserved.
Copyright © 1998 by Roger Crawford.
BOOK DESIGN BY JESSICA SHATAN.

No part of this book may be reproduced or transmitted in any form or by any
means, electronic or mechanical, including photocopying, recording, or by
any information storage and retrieval system, without permission in writing
from the publisher. For information address: Bantam Books.

Library of Congress Cataloging-in-Publication Data
Crawford, Roger, 1960–
How high can you bounce? : turn your setbacks into comebacks /
Roger Crawford.
p.   cm.
Includes bibliographical references.
ISBN 0-553-10461-6
1. Success—Psychological aspects.   2. Resilience (Personality trait)   I. Title.
BF637.S8C73   1998
158.1—dc21   97-36689
CIP

Published simultaneously in the United States and Canada

Bantam Books are published by Bantam Books, a division of Bantam
Doubleday Dell Publishing Group, Inc. Its trademark, consisting of the
words "Bantam Books" and the portrayal of a rooster, is Registered in
U.S. Patent and Trademark Office and in other countries. Marca Registrada. Bantam Books, 1540 Broadway, New York, New York 10036.

PRINTED IN THE UNITED STATES OF AMERICA

BVG   10   9   8   7   6   5   4   3   2   1

This book is dedicated to
Donna and Alexa, my angels.

CONTENTS

My gratitude . . .

To the individuals and organizations whose real-life struggles and subsequent victories are chronicled in this book. You are the real heroes, and my life is richer because of you.

To Eleanor Dugan. When I began this project, you said your contribution would be as my "Grammar Granny," but you have been so much more than that. Your wisdom, warm charm, and belief in this book made the process so rewarding.

To my dear friends and literary agents, Michael Larsen and Elizabeth Pomada. You saw the possibilities in this book at its inception, and your energy and brilliant creativity made my dream a reality. Cheers!

To my editor, Toni Burbank. Thank you for your inspiration, vision, and encouragement. You helped me rescue my own resilience on several occasions. I feel so fortunate to have had the opportunity of working with the best.

To Bill and Sheila Bethel for introducing me to Eleanor Dugan and Michael Larsen. You were the springboard for this book.

To the many individuals who generously contributed their time and valuable feedback on the manuscript, a heartfelt thank-you. These include: Jill Coogan, Tony and Micky Fisher, Cheryl Koenig, Laurel Sarmento, Phil Scott, and my valued friends and mentors in the Speakers' Roundtable.

To the hundreds of corporations, associations, and school districts that have given me the privilege of sharing my message, I am most appreciative.

To my precious daughter, Alexa. This book was conceived about the same time you were. Our friends were in awe when, at age two, you could say the word "resilience"! I will always cherish the memories of your tucking a stuffed animal in my luggage before I left on a trip so I wouldn't be lonely. Your many hugs and kisses sustained my resilience during the long hours of writing. I am blessed to be your daddy.

To my incredible wife, Donna. I want to thank you for your love, patience, enthusiasm, and sense of humor. Halfway through this project, you laughingly suggested a title change to *How I Had a Nervous Breakdown Writing a Book on Resilience*. You have been a true partner on this book, serving as initial editor, reading and rereading every line, and your suggestions improved the manuscript immensely. You make life so sweet.

How High Can You Bounce?

BOUNCE OR BREAK?

If you put a golf ball in the freezer until the core gets very cold, it loses its resilience. No matter how hard you hit it, it's not going to go far. Even after the outside has warmed up and the ball seems completely normal, it won't perform like a regular ball. And if the ball gets cold enough, it will splinter on impact.

People are like that. They can look pretty much alike, come from similar backgrounds, and go through similar experiences. Yet, in the same situation, one person soars and another comes up short, one person flourishes and another is devastated.

Those who soar through life have resilience. Their resilient core transforms the momentum of life's many blows into speed and distance. The same forces that shatter others are what keep them going.

Resilient people regain their stability more quickly in difficult situations, and stay physically and emotionally healthy during periods of stress and uncertainty. They stay hopeful and optimistic when others give up. They rebound from adversity even stronger than before.

A high level of resilience is a great thing to have. It makes our lives richer, more productive, happier, and more successful. But how do we get it? We're all born with some resilience or we wouldn't be here. A few charmed individuals seem to have gotten more than the rest of us, surviving with a smile everything that life throws at them.

The rest of us have a conscious choice. We can allow ourselves to freeze up, calcify, to slowly become brittle and inflexible like frail old trees waiting to blow down in the next strong wind. Or we can take steps to develop and maintain our resilience. Fortunately, resilience is a skill you can learn.

If you're alive, you're going to face challenges and hardships. Many of mine are obvious. At birth, I faced a physical challenge that affected all four limbs. The medical explanation was "ectrodactylism." My preferred term is "inconvenienced." Basically, my hands aren't fully developed. A thumb extends from my right wrist, and a thumb and pinky from my left wrist. One foot has three toes. My other leg was underdeveloped and was amputated below the knee when I was five so I could wear an artificial leg. Suddenly I had the agility to walk and run. What an incredible turning point in my life!

Has this physical challenge limited me? Of course. I can't eat with chopsticks or play "Chopsticks." That's one of the realities of my life and yours: We must accept what we cannot change.

As soon as I developed the necessary mobility, athletics (especially tennis) became a positive influence in my life. I captained my high school tennis team and had a singles record of forty-seven wins, six losses. In college, I became the first person with a physical challenge affecting two or more limbs to participate in Division I NCAA athletics. I'm proud of this accomplishment, but I didn't do it alone. Loving, supportive parents, excellent coaching, and some God-given ability made it possible.

Was I any more "handicapped" than someone able-bodied who is disadvantaged by poverty, a dysfunctional family, or a negative self-image? I don't believe so. It's the invisible handicaps—attitudinal, spiritual, or emotional—that are the most painful and difficult to overcome. As an objective self-observer, I've noticed that the handicaps that limited me were self-imposed and from the neck up. Many people I meet have faced difficulties less obvious but far more severe than mine. I'm not unique. The drama of my life is probably very similar to yours.

Because of my experiences, my passion for learning, and a keen interest in human potential, I began a speaking and training business. My clients now include many Fortune 500 companies and numerous trade and professional associations. My career has taken me to all fifty states and over sixteen countries around the world. Every day I feel as if I am making a positive difference in the lives of others.

But this book is not about my life, it's about yours. It's about nine ways to make yourself stronger, more powerful, and more resilient. In sports, in business, and in life, I've always been fascinated by the enormous difference that resilience makes. Is there a way to tell who will thrive and who will fail? Is there a formula for building resilient organizations or raising resilient children? And can we *learn* to be more resilient? After studying hundreds of organizations and talking with thousands of exceptional people, I'm convinced that the answer to all these questions is yes!

In this book, you will be reading stories about highly resilient people—people who have been challenged and who have emerged even wiser and better equipped to manage the future. At first you may think, "Oh, I could never do that!" But how do you know? These are all ordinary people who have been able to tap the extraordinary resources within themselves. This can be your life as well!

We can't control which difficulties we'll encounter, but we *can* control how we'll respond to them. We can choose to be victims or victors, winners or whiners, optimistic or pessimistic.

We all need resilience on a daily basis, not just in times of catastrophe. The cumulative effect of everyday stress of family, job, and even traffic jams can be nearly as hard to deal with as great tragedy. When something goes wrong, do we see it as further evidence of life's unfairness and futility? Or can we find the opportunities for growth? Once we make this crucial attitude shift, a resilient life is within our grasp. We have seized the power. We can now convert mountains into molehills and discover abilities and internal boldness that we never knew existed.

Your Road Map to Resilience

I was driving back from a speaking engagement in Canada. As I entered the United States, a border guard stopped me and asked to see my driver's license. Then he asked me three questions.

"Sir, where are you coming from?"

"Vancouver," I told him.

"How long have you been there?"

"Two days," I replied.

"And where are you going, sir?"

"Seattle, Washington."

I drove off down the highway, thinking about what I planned to do later that day. Suddenly I experienced such a mental blast that I did one of those double takes that they do in cartoons. The words of the border guard came back to me and blocked out everything else from my mind. It was an analogy of resilience so powerful and perfect that I had difficulty concentrating on the road. I pulled over and stopped so I could write it down.

Every day since then, I've asked myself these same three questions:

Where are you coming from? *(Your attitudes)*

How you explain your past experiences to yourself reveals the beliefs that shape your reaction to every event, happy or unhappy. Your attitudes are the window through which you see your life experience.

When nonresilient people ask themselves "Where am I coming from?" they look at their past and see problems, failure, and fragility. They seek evidence that supports their nonresilience. But when resilient people ask themselves "Where am I coming from?" they look at their past and see solutions, strength, and inspiration. They actively seek evidence that supports their resilience. *We become what we dwell on.*

Resilient people realize that it's impossible to see the full value of adversity until it is behind us. Understanding and wisdom come after an event, not before, and hindsight is twenty-twenty. You can forge your images of past events, both good and bad, into a positive, consistent vision of resilience.

How long have you been there? *(Your self-image)*

Your reputation with yourself is never static. It fluctuates daily, influenced by internal and external circumstances. Resilient people conduct regular self-image appraisals; they take responsibility for their feelings, resources, and any necessary course-corrections.

Nonresilient people tend to avoid self-evaluation; it can provide uncomfortable information. However, a lethargic spirit can respond to self-evaluation the same way a lethargic body responds to exercise—with renewed energy. Self-reflection strengthens our resilience and our ability to shape our future.

Where are you going? *(Your motivations)*

The power to accomplish great things is strongest when we get our attitudes, self-image, and sense of purpose into alignment. Resilient people have a clarity of vision that keeps them focused and functioning during difficult situations. They have a unique, highly personal definition of "success" that insulates them from the everyday wear and tear that grinds others down.

Motivation is self-generated, a combination of your physical energy and mental attitude. Since the software drives the hardware, your mind initiates your actions. Other people can stimulate you and guide you, but only you can motivate yourself.

These three questions form the framework of this book. Your answers to them become the bulwarks of your resilient core. You can't get powerful answers until you ask powerful questions.

Your Nine Keys to Resilience

Strengthening your resilience is like strengthening your muscles. Both can be accomplished with a program of regular stretching and exercises. Attitude stretching requires no special clothing or expensive equipment, just awareness. Here are your nine keys to improving your resilience:

1. Believe Success Is Possible. Resilient thinking is the foundation of resilience. Even if you weren't "born resilient," you can *learn* to reframe negative events into positive challenges, giving yourself extra energy and endurance. Start by paying attention to how you talk to yourself each day.

2. Flex Your Humor Muscles. Flexibility is essential for controlling stress, increasing business opportunities, improving personal relationships, and dealing with change. How can you limber up? When you avoid immobilizing perfectionism and give yourself permission to notice the genuine humor that is all around us, you automatically increase your flexibility and vitality.

3. Bank on Your Past. Draw strength and inspiration from what you've done and what has happened to you. We're often told, "Don't look back" and "Don't dwell on the past," but when you know what to recall and use the information positively, you can tap some of your most valuable assets.

4. Stay Hungry. The most basic human instinct is a powerful tool for maintaining resilience. Learn the difference between money and true wealth, and where and how to direct your hunger for knowledge, for adventure, and for positive personal relationships.

5. Use All Your Resources. Make a realistic inventory of your many assets. As you compile your catalog, you'll discover some surprising and important skills and resources that you never realized you had.

6. Seize Responsibility. Decide what you can control. Then take responsibility for it. What an important life skill, yet non-resilient people fail to grasp it and feel overwhelmed much of the time. When you learn how to take these two decisive steps, you put yourself in control, no matter what life throws at you.

7. Harness the Power of Purpose. Having clear goals and an Action Plan to reach them is absolutely mandatory for success. "The Five E's of Goal Setting" will show you an efficient new way to plan and achieve.

8. Develop Your Inborn Leadership. Everything you say and do also affects the resilience of others. No matter who you are and what position you hold at the moment, you become a powerful leader at work, at home, and in your community when you learn to share your resilience.

9. Embrace Challenges. Learn the difference between planning and preparation, and how the resilient prepare for life's many challenges. Even when fate delivers an unexpected blow, you'll be able to draw on your storehouse of resilience to identify the new and exciting opportunities that await you.

Each of the nine chapters in this book shows you strategies for acquiring one of these nine skills. You'll learn how to stay in optimal mental shape by nourishing and exercising these resilient qualities each day, the same way you nourish and exercise your body.

As you strengthen your skills, you are building an invincible core of resilience that will always be there for you to draw on. Too often, when people suffer a major loss, they also lose their sense of identity and purpose in life. But with a resilient core, you keep a clear inner vision of your strength and flexibility in the face of challenges.

Resilience Is a Choice

My focus on resilience started some years ago with a telephone call from a stranger. The man on the other end of the line said he'd seen a newspaper article about my tennis victories. He told me he thought we had something in common, and he'd like to meet me. Intrigued, I agreed to get together at a nearby restaurant. He described himself: six two with a mustache and curly hair. I got there early and, when I spotted him coming in the door, I stood up and went over to shake his hand. He extended his arm and I realized that his hands were almost identical to mine.

At first, as we talked, I was excited about meeting someone so similar to myself but older, someone who might serve as a mentor for me. Instead, what I found was someone with a bitter, pessimistic attitude who blamed all of life's disappointments and failures on his anatomy.

I soon recognized that our lives and attitudes couldn't have been more different. Where my parents had turned out to cheer me on at sporting events, his parents had kept him sheltered at home. He had never held a job for long, and he was sure this was because of "discrimination"—certainly not because (as he admitted) he was constantly late, frequently absent, and failed to take any responsibility for his work. His attitude was, "The world owes me," and his problem was that the world disagreed. He was even somewhat angry with me because I didn't share his despair.

We kept in touch for several years, until it dawned on me that even if some miracle were suddenly to give him a perfect body, his unhappiness and lack of success wouldn't change. He would still be at the same place in his life.

This chance encounter with someone so similar and yet so different changed my life. I suddenly understood that *the quality of our lives is governed not by outward circumstances, but by the choices we make.* This is what inspired me to find out why some of us are able to make positive choices in the face of setbacks and losses, while others are defeated by life's inevitable challenges—why some of us develop a high degree of resilience and soar, while others thud to the ground like the frozen golf ball.

I hope this book encourages you to notice and reinforce your resilient spirit when you are feeling strong and everything is going great. I hope it will also help and inspire you when you're confronting difficulties.

In my office I have a handsome bronze torch, its top blackened by the flame that once burned there. Circling the rim are three Latin words:

citius • altius • fortius
"swifter, higher, stronger"

On a Thursday afternoon in 1984, I had the great honor of carrying that Olympic torch through San Francisco on one leg of its journey from Athens to Los Angeles. It was about 5:00 PM, and the crowds lining the streets were joined by many more people just leaving work. They all cheered me on as I ran past Union Square and uphill along Grant Avenue. I've never forgotten the thrill and inspiration of that day and the three words engraved on that torch. The ideas in this book are intended to help you light your own internal torch, so that you will be *swifter,* bounce *higher,* and grow *stronger.* This is the essence of your resilience.

PART ONE

"Where Are You Coming From?"

YOUR ATTITUDES

The pilot's definition of *attitude* is as relevant for living as it is for flying. In aviation, attitude is the relationship of the plane to the horizon. An instrument in the cockpit, the attitude sensor, measures how far the plane is leaning one way or the other—but passengers rarely get to see it unless they ride some of the smaller commuter airlines, as I do. (You know the planes I'm, talking about. You ask for a window seat and the gate agent replies, "I'm sorry, the captain already has that one.") When these small planes run into turbulence, the pilots have a saying: "Keep your nose in the blue." As long as you keep your nose aimed at a point above the horizon, you won't crash. In other words, *attitude determines altitude*. The same is true for people.

We are the results of our choices, not our circumstances. It is not events that define our lives, but our attitudes toward these events and how we respond to them. Other people can try to control our circumstances, but they can't control our *attitudes* unless we let them. We invent and create our lives every day with the choices that we make. Our lives are the product of our attitudes.

This is good news because it puts us in the driver's seat. There are some things we can try to influence but that ultimately we can't control: other people's attitudes and actions, weather, the passing of time, etc. There are some things we can control: our values, feelings, thoughts, and actions, and our *attitudes* toward other people's attitudes and actions, weather, passing time, etc.

Choosing how we view and respond to events is called *selective perception*. When there is something we can't change, we can choose to feel frustrated, miserable, or hopeless. Or we can select an alternate perception. We can choose to see the unchangeable as a useful tool, as inspiring and energizing, or as irrelevant and amusing.

Your First Set of Keys

These first three chapters are about *attitudes* because they are the foundation of your resilience.

> **1. Believe Success Is Possible.** Flip this power switch to get started.
> **2. Flex Your Humor Muscles.** Use humor for strength, endurance, and buoyancy.
> **3. Bank on Your Past.** Recognize the assets you already have.

Our attitudes are a set of beliefs that predispose us to react to people or situations in a particular way. Often we can't control our experiences, but we all have the power to decide on our emotional responses to them. When we learn to control our thoughts, we take a major step toward controlling our resilience! Our attitudes create our perceptions, and our perceptions shape our reality about who we are and what we can become.

Early in this century, a French psychologist demonstrated the power of perception with this proposition: Take a thick plank a foot wide and twenty feet long. Lay it flat on the ground and ask people to walk the length of it without stepping off. Almost everyone will be able to do so easily. Now place the plank between two church spires several hundred feet in the air and repeat the request. Few will agree to try. The plank is still a foot wide and twenty feet long. Nothing has changed except the perception of danger.

Unless you have a strong, resilient attitude about the world around you and how you relate to it, you'll shrink from challenges and make yourself vulnerable to being crushed by chance events. Your resilience starts with fortifying your positive attitudes and rethinking the negative ones that are holding you back. These first three keys offer you the tools you'll need to build your foundation of resilience.

1

Believe Success Is Possible

LEARN TO THINK RESILIENTLY

One afternoon I returned home from a series of speaking engagements and my wife, Donna, met me at the San Francisco Airport. I'd just missed a world-record four plane connections in one day. This was on top of a microphone malfunction during an important speech. I have to admit that, at that point, I had gotten into a pretty negative state of mind. My attitude was, "What *else* can go wrong?"

My wife was very understanding. "You go get your bags," she said, "I'll get the car, and we'll go out for a nice relaxing dinner." I went to the baggage carousel and waited. And waited. Do you know that sinking feeling when the carousel screeches to a halt and you are the only person still standing there? I went to file a claim and I admit I was less than optimistic.

The man at the counter asked my name. "Roger Crawford," I

replied. "Address?" I told him. Then he asked my occupation. "I'm a speaker and writer on the subject of resilience," I said. *"What's it to you?"*

Outside at the curb my wife was waiting patiently. "Donna, give me those keys," I growled. "I'm driving." We drove out of the airport and right into rush-hour traffic. "Where did all these people come from!" I snarled. At that moment, my wife turned to look at me with *that* look. If you're married you'll understand what I mean. It's the look that only a spouse can give, one that is developed and refined over the years into nonverbal communication at its finest.

"Roger Crawford, I have something you need to listen to," she said. She grabbed a cassette from the glove compartment and shoved it into the tape player. Suddenly I heard something that immediately changed my mood. It was a powerful voice that grabbed my attention with its enthusiasm and conviction. And I heard this voice—my own voice—saying, "I'd rather have one leg and a positive attitude than two legs and a negative attitude, every single time . . ."

As we begin this book, I would like you to take time to listen to your own tape. Start by conducting an attitude appraisal. A resilient attitude isn't developed overnight with a single decision. It is a sustained commitment that requires personal discipline and awareness. Appraising your attitude is not a onetime event. Resilient people do it on a daily basis.

The Power of Optimism

You can't be resilient without optimism, without having a fundamental conviction that, somehow, sooner or later, things are going to turn out successfully. I believe that optimism is far more important in life than giftedness. It is the core of resilient thinking and the forerunner of all the skills needed for accomplishment, happiness, and resilience.

Optimism is often called "hope" by philosophers, "faith" by clergymen, "hardiness" by the medical profession, and "resilience" by most of the rest of us. First, let me tell you what optimism *isn't*.

It isn't a Pollyanna attitude or wishful thinking. It doesn't mean ignoring life's realities while waiting around for good things to happen. Optimism isn't gullibility or blind trust. It isn't trying to draw to an inside straight or investing your retirement fund with a fast-talking banana-oil salesman.

Here's what optimism *is*. It's a belief that life will be, in the long run, more good than bad, that even when bad things happen, the good will eventually outbalance them. It's also the belief that nearly every difficulty conceals some potential benefit if only we have the skill to find it.

BOUNCE HIGHER TIP

Indulging in negative thinking is one of the most expensive hobbies you can have.

Optimism is expecting that most things will work out to a successful completion, and even more important, that you have the power to contribute to that outcome. Adversity is temporary and can be remedied through your efforts and the assistance of others. When you expect a positive outcome, you're prepared emotionally and physically for the rigors of life. When you make this kind of thinking a habit, you can roll with the punches whenever they are thrown at you.

Even when a positive outcome is unlikely or impossible, optimists choose to view the negative payoff in the same way that a judo master views an attack; they convert the negative energy to positive uses by developing or expanding some productive aspect of themselves.

As humans, we're capable of dealing with only one dominant thought at a time. Therefore, it's impossible to be both resilient and pessimistic simultaneously. You have to choose, and you become what you think about most. People who study the human mind call it the *principle of dominant thought*.

In his book *Illusions*, Richard Bach says, "Argue for your

limitations and they are yours." If we view ourselves as under-achievers, we will make sure our lives reflect that negative view. When something good happens, a pessimistic person is often un-comfortable, anxious, and eager to "get back where I belong." On the other hand, if we see ourselves as able to achieve, we'll do whatever it takes to make our mental picture match reality. And we'll be more venturesome, spontaneous, and creative when we run into a setback. What we think, what we visualize, and what we forecast is what we ultimately become.

Resilient Thinking Versus "Positive Thinking"

Resilient thinking is different from positive thinking. Positive thinking is a component of resilience, but resilient thinking takes you one step farther. It is tough-minded and reality-based. Often people think that all they need to achieve their hopes and dreams is a positive belief system. Positive thinking has tremendous bene-fits, but sometimes it's not enough.

With resilient thinking, you focus on the positive without deny-ing the negative. Resilient thinkers never pretend that things are different from how they really are. They can see the stumbling blocks, but they choose the stepping-stones.

Recognize both the good and the bad in our world, but look for what's right, not what's wrong. It's a case of "what you see is what you'll get." Unfortunately, negativity sells. Catastrophes and ex-amples of human cruelty make good headlines, but that's because they're so unusual. We tend to ignore all the good things that hap-pen because they're common. We need to guard constantly against being dragged down by the complainers and doomsayers around us. It's not just the headlines, it can be a coworker or a neighbor. Negativity can be catching!

I believe that 97 percent of the people in this world are good-hearted and try to do the right thing. It's the other 3 percent that get the press. Resilient thinkers view the darkness as necessary shadow to emphasize the light that surrounds them. They don't say "I'm happy" or "I'm successful" if they're not. Instead, they remain certain that things can and will be better.

Positive thinking: I feel happy. *(But I really don't.)*
Resilient thinking: Right now I feel lousy, but I have it in my power to be happy.

Positive thinking: I am successful. *(But I'm not.)*
Resilient thinking: Today I had a setback, but I can turn it around.

See the difference? Resilient people don't have to misinterpret their situation. We've all known someone who thought positively, did everything right, but still encountered hardships. Thinking positively cannot shield us from every disappointment, unhappiness, or misfortune. But when you use resilient thinking to focus on the positive, you discover you feel energized and can uncover possibilities you didn't notice before. This energy and insight gives you a huge advantage for dealing with setbacks. Focusing on the positive is the essence of resilient thinking.

You Are What You Think

Your subconscious mind starts out inherently optimistic. If you doubt this, watch what happens when someone tells a child, "Don't put beans in your ear." Chances are they will soon make a trip to the doctor for bean removal. This is because the subconscious mind doesn't accept the negative "don't." It concentrates on the rest of the message.

Messages that are framed with a negative may communicate the opposite of what is intended—"Don't eat junk food." "Don't drive too fast." "Don't drop that." "Don't fail." Our minds instantly focus on french fries or the potential for fumbling! The moral: Whether you're communicating with others or with yourself, frame every idea as positively as possible.

NOT: I won't fall below my sales quota this month.
BUT: I'll meet my sales quota this month.

NOT: Don't eat junk food.
BUT: Eat all those fabulously delicious foods that nourish and nurture the body.

NOT: Stop doing that!
BUT: Do this!

Whenever I talk to a group about resilience, usually someone in the audience stays behind to ask for advice. They know somone or live with someone who had a difficult experience and now seems trapped in negativity. One woman told me that ever since her husband had lost his job, he treated her badly and just moped around the house. "What can I do to cheer him up?" she asked.

Before I could make any suggestions, I needed to know more. Was he a positive, high-achieving, vibrant person one day and totally devastated the next? Was he fine before he lost his job? "Oh, no, he was pretty nasty then too," she admitted. "Now he has something to blame it on."

Clearly this gentleman's unhappiness was the result of negativity, not unemployment. If he'd been gainfully employed, he'd have found something else to fuel his pessimism. I regretfully told his wife that no one can change another person's attitude. We can support, encourage, and model optimism, but they alone decide what to focus on. His resilience was determined by his choices, not by his circumstances.

BOUNCE HIGHER TIP

*Your state of mind determines
your state of resilience.*

Use Optimism as a Power Tool

If you're not already an incurable optimist, is it really worth the effort to change your attitude and habits? As you consider your answer, look at the advantages of a resilient, optimistic attitude.

You're healthier

Thousands of medical studies in recent decades have shown how people's attitudes can profoundly affect their bodies. These studies indicate that optimists are consistently healthier and hardier than pessimists. (One reason may be that optimists feel in control of themselves and their destinies, and so they may use more conscious, effective measures to avoid illness and accidents.) The good news is that you don't have to visit a physician to change your attitude. You can conduct your own mental checkup.

You're happier

Optimists and pessimists have one thing in common: Sooner or later both will be proved right. It's the interims that are different. When things go right, optimists are happy and pessimists are not unhappy. When things are rotten, optimists are unhappy, but pessimists, who should be delighted that their worst fears have been realized, are even more unhappy. Optimists are not happy all the time, but pessimists are *never* happy. So, which would you rather be?

You achieve more

Did you know that a high level of optimism can predict achievement? Mark Warshauer, vice president of Compucom, told me about the connection he's observed between optimism and sales success. "I evaluate prospective sales professionals by asking them to tell me about their past achievements and failures," he says. "If they dwell on setbacks and blame others for past mistakes, that's a clear indicator of nonresilience. If they focus on their triumphs and take full responsibility for missteps, I know they possess optimism and its all-important by-product, resilience." Success is rarely achieved unless we're sure it is within our grasp.

Let me tell you about a remarkable woman who had this "I can" attitude. In the late 1980s, I was interviewed by Dorothy Fulltime, a newscaster at Cleveland's WEWS-TV. This was a big thrill for me because I remembered watching her when I was a child. Among Dorothy Fulltime's many distinctions was that she had been a working journalist longer than anyone alive. In her earlier days, she had interviewed many world leaders, including Franklin Delano Roosevelt and Joseph Stalin. She was ninety-one years old when she interviewed me. Soon after, I read that she had just signed a new *five-year* contract with the TV station! Fulfilling her contract would take her to the age of ninety-six. Now, *that's* positive expectancy!

So, optimistic, resilient individuals are happier, healthier, and achieve more than pessimists. They are more able to resist injury and stress, and they recover faster and better than unfit individuals. They also do better personally and professionally. But you can't just decide to become resilient overnight. The best time to stockpile your resilience isn't when you need it the most; it's right now.

HOW DO WE BECOME RESILIENT THINKERS?

Master the Language of Resilience

Two words that will jeopardize your resilience: *If only* . . . When people have lost their bounce, they can use up their precious remaining energy with self-talk about lost chances: "If only I had done things differently." "If only I had made a better decision." "If only . . ." It's all too easy to become trapped in a cycle of negative language.

The resilient consciously use a different vocabulary, a "language of resilience," to explain events to themselves. When they catch themselves feeling negative, they turn *if only* into *next time*—"*Next time* I'll be better informed." "*Next time* I'll be more prepared." *If only* focuses on past failures and erodes resilience. *Next time* focuses you on future successes and builds your resilience.

BOUNCE HIGHER TIP

Whenever you catch yourself saying "If only,"
make a conscious switch to "Next time."

People in an unresilient state blame themselves for every setback. Then they tell themselves that the resulting negativity is going to be permanent and will infect every other aspect of their lives. But when people feel resilient, they tend to see the same failures and disasters as resulting from outside forces, a temporary problem that applies to only one aspect of their lives.

Unresilient language: It's all my fault.
Resilient language: That's one factor I had no control over.

Unresilient language: It's going to be this way forever.
Resilient language: It's just temporary.

The reverse is true for happy events. The unresilient see positive occurrences as beyond their control, temporary, and touching on only one part of their lives.

Unresilient language: This one time I finally got lucky.
Resilient language: I've got what it takes!

Unresilient language: It will never last.
Resilient language: This is just the beginning!

The resilient see positive events as direct accomplishments or as growing out of the positive nature of their lives. These good things are incorporated into their life pictures and they don't focus on their fear of losing them. Even experiencing these good events briefly contributes to their reservoirs of resilience and optimism: "It's out there and I can have it again." The unresilient see the loss of a good thing as proof of their unworthiness or failure.

The unresilient see every triumph as pure luck or caused by someone else's efforts, but they blame themselves for negative events. Now, that's some trap! They also see themselves at the center of the active universe. That means that every bus door that slams in their faces proves the world is conspiring to make their lives miserable, and each paper cut is a cosmic judgment for perceived inadequacies. They may protest, "Why me?" or "What next?" but they already know the answer.

Resilient thinkers reverse the process, feeling that they can affect the positive aspects of their lives, while refusing to feel guilty about negative events they can't control. This gives them a real edge when bad things happen.

Negative fact: I broke it.
Unresilient language: I'm so clumsy.
Resilient language: Today I've been dropping things.

Negative fact: My boss bawled me out.
Unresilient language: My boss is a @#!
Resilient language: She's sure in a bad mood right now.

When we're unresilient, we see a single negative event as proof positive of eternal inadequacy, but if we're in a resilient mode, it is just a temporary glitch.

Negative fact: My boss is furious about my mistake.
Unresilient conclusion: I'm incompetent.
Resilient conclusion: I'd better double-check my figures next time.

Negative fact: My boyfriend lied to me about dating Susie.
Unresilient conclusion: All men are rats.
Resilient conclusion: Sam is not ready to commit to a relationship.

Whenever we're feeling highly resilient, we also see ourselves as deserving the good things that come our way.

Positive fact: I won that game.
Unresilient conclusion: My opponent had an off day.
Resilient conclusion: I'm a healthy, fit person and a pretty good player.

Positive fact: My boss liked my report.
Unresilient conclusion: He must have been in a good mood this time.
Resilient conclusion: I do my job well.

To maintain your resilience, label positive situations with lavish generalities that apply to all areas of your life, but be very specific and limiting when you talk to yourself about negative events.

Life's problems are like small fires in a large building. If we can shut a door and confine the problem to one area, it is less likely to spread. But if all the doors are open, the problems can feed on each other and build into one huge inferno of negativism and hopelessness.

Listen to Your Tape

Which would you rather be, powerful or pitiful? Would you prefer to take charge and take off? Or just take it? To act or to react? Nothing can devastate us without our permission. We can choose to describe any situation in resilient language, to replace "negative tapes" with positive ones.

How you talk to yourself affects your level of resilience. Do you use resilient language? Or unresilient language?

Unresilient language:	Resilient language:
failure	obstacle
downfall	setback
ruin	learning experience
disaster	hurdle
calamity	opportunity
catastrophe	big break
misfortune	possibility
trouble	challenge
lucky break	well-earned opportunity
fate	results of my efforts
destiny	payoff for my hard work

The next time you catch yourself using unresilient words or phrases, switch to resilient language.

Instead of: Why didn't I . . .
Switch to: Next time I'm going to . . .

Instead of: I'm no good at that.
Switch to: Right now that's not among my top skills, but I'm terrific at . . .

Using the language of resilience, you can literally talk yourself into greater endurance and optimism.

Monitor Your Mental Diet

Just as we watch what nourishment we put into our bodies, we need to watch what nourishment we put into our minds. Resilience and courage depend on the quality and content of our thoughts. Positive thoughts inspire us, keeping us flexible and strong. Negative words leave us uninspired, brittle, and weak.

The religious and political leader Mohandas Gandhi, who mod-

eled nonviolence as a tool for social change, knew the importance
of positive input. He said:

> Keep my words positive, because my words become behaviors.
> Keep my behaviors positive, because my behaviors become
> habits.
> Keep my habits positive, because my habits become my values.
> And keep my values positive, because they become my destiny.

Physically fit people understand the importance of good nutrition
and exercise. After a strenuous workout, they replenish their bodies
with nourishing food. The same is true for people who stay in optimal mental shape. Building optimism and mental resilience requires
the same careful nourishment that building physical resilience does.
We need the right mental nutrition—all through the day.

Breakfast of Champions—As you plan the hours ahead, see
yourself achieving, and see yourself solving problems in a positive,
productive day.

Power Lunch—Use this time to evaluate your progress. If you
had a difficult morning, focus on your strengths and solutions as
you anticipate a much better afternoon.

Gourmet Dinner—We gain insight and understanding from looking back. Take a careful and honest look at your day. What wisdom
can you take from it?

Late-Night Snack—Count the blessings of the day. Practice an
attitude of gratitude.

Five years from now you're going to be exactly the same person
you are today—except for the people you have chosen to be with,
the experiences you have sought out, the books you picked to

read, the films and television programs you selected to watch, and the messages you decided to send yourself. These conscious and unconscious choices will shape you more profoundly than any chance happenings, good or bad.

BOUNCE HIGHER TIP

Discouragement is a choice.
So is optimism.

That's why optimistic people monitor everything they put in their minds. The experiences we choose to drive our lives are like the software that drives a computer. The quality and power can vary tremendously. Computer programmers have a motto: "Garbage in, garbage out." You can't expect a quality product without quality ingredients.

Of course, a consciously negative attitude is sometimes necessary as a reality check. If you're about to drive through a desert, it's better to overestimate how much gas and water you'll need. And who wants a cockeyed optimist as an air-traffic controller or an anesthesiologist? A cautious attitude is essential for any job where safety judgments are made or where you must prepare for the worst. Happily, it is possible to perform the most arduous, nitpicking tasks with a positive frame of mind. It's all a matter of *attitude*.

Join a Mental Health Club

Some of us can successfully exercise alone, and some of us do better when we work out with others. The same is true for mental health. If you've lost your job unexpectedly, you may be in a state of shock. If you've been rejected by someone you love, you may be feeling unlovable. Even common everyday knocks can wear you down until you feel you need a boost. At times like these, resilient people join a Mental Health Club. The first rule of membership is to check your negative attitudes at the door.

Seek out a place where you'll be surrounded by optimistic, supportive people who will celebrate your uniqueness and triumphs. This may be within your network of friends, at your place of worship, or in a formal support group. Identify "workout" areas where you can share ideas and solve problems creatively. Through the example and wisdom of others who have faced similar obstacles, you'll regain your confidence and self-regard. Your "club" can provide you with precious assistance and receive your input in return. When you see others benefiting from your knowledge and caring, you fortify your self-image as a resilient achiever.

One of my "clubs" is a professional organization called the Speakers' Roundtable. The synergy created among the members is both uplifting and energizing, and the extraordinary mental boost I get from my colleagues is priceless. When you want to maintain your bounce, you can find strength in such partnerships at your own Mental Health Club.

Exercise Your Attitudes

Some people never try to increase their skills and improve their performance because they believe the effort required is too overwhelming. But the distance between resilience and nonresilience is usually very short: It's the distance between our ears.

Here's an example from my tennis-playing days. Suppose you are playing a match and expect to win 55 percent of the points and lose 45 percent. That's a 10-percent spread. What are your chances of winning the match? Most people guess 55 percent, but the real answer will surprise you: 91 percent. If you played 100 times, you should win 91 of the matches! Consider the implications of this. Just a small edge—10 percent in points—will have a big effect— 91 percent—on the number of matches won.

If you think of all the points in the match as being worth the same, it equalizes the impact of each point. Even after losing an apparently critical point, good players understand that every point counts. You can lose nearly half the points and still be confident you'll win the match.

Suppose you want to win all the time. What percentage point spread would you need to win at least 99 percent of your matches? The answer is about 20 percent. This means you'd be nearly unbeatable if you could consistently win 60 percent of the points. In the same way, just small incremental improvements in our lives add up to a huge difference.

Improving your attitude involves the same steps as improving your body, with the same possibilities for backsliding. Have you ever resolved to start a new exercise program and then slipped back into your old ways from force of habit? Strengthening your attitudinal muscles presents the same challenges.

Here's how to keep from slipping. Starting right now, establish just one attitude goal, one that you can measure on a daily basis. For example, just for today, eliminate those self-deprecating remarks that subconsciously fuel pessimism. No more muttering to yourself, "Boy, was that a dumb thing to say," or "Now I've really blown it!" Do this for one day. Then another and another, until it becomes a habit. Attitude fitness, like physical fitness, requires lifestyle changes. Don't try to change everything at once. Start small and grow, constantly reevaluating and changing strategies if necessary.

Build a Gratitude Filter

When we begin to acknowledge what we do have in our lives, we suddenly notice possibilities we've been overlooking. The late Dr. Norman Vincent Peale called this expanded awareness "the attitude of gratitude."

Go get a piece of paper and a pencil and write down everything you're grateful for. If you're feeling cynical, your greatest challenge may be persuading yourself to try it, but I guarantee you'll be surprised at the positive results.

But what about people who wake up to real misery, to life without health, shelter, food, or the people they love? They couldn't possibly have anything to be optimistic about, right? But resilient people do. Once when I was speaking in Germany, I met a successful young businesswoman who had grown up under communism. I asked her how she had maintained her optimism when life seemed to hold so few options. She replied, "My father always said, 'Be thankful for what we have, and at least we're not Bulgarians.'" Now, I certainly don't recommend disparaging anyone else to maintain your resilience, but being thankful for something—anything—is the first step to building resilience.

Learn to celebrate Thanksgiving 365 days a year! It's human nature to take the blessings in life for granted. Can you remember wanting something desperately, getting it, and then barely being aware of it a few months later?

Start noticing the remarkable things in your life now, both obvious and less obvious. Build a gratitude filter to catch all the good things that happen. Then, whenever you're feeling less than resilient, stop and identify all you've got to be grateful for. Your positive thoughts will crowd hurt and despair out of your mind. You won't have time for regret, envy, or disappointment.

PROFILE

Phil Butler

When I need an extra reminder about the connection between optimism and resilience, I think of Phil Butler. Phil graduated from Annapolis and became a Navy light-attack carrier pilot who seemed to have the world by the tail. Then he was shot down on a bombing mission over North Vietnam. He spent four days trying to escape through the jungle before he was captured and imprisoned. Each day in his cell he hoped that tomorrow might bring freedom. He maintained this hope for eight years! Phil managed not only to survive but also to accomplish the POW mission—"to return with honor."

Phil told me how the prisoners were kept separate to break their spirits so they could be used for political propaganda. Despite this isolation, they managed to develop and use a secret method of communicating. They created a tap code based on assigning letters to a five-by-five box grid, rather than using traditional Morse code, which might have been deciphered by the guards. Messages could be sent by tapping lightly on the wall or even by the swishes of a broom while sweeping the courtyard. Phil and the others would sweep out jokes and stories to entertain all the other prisoners.

New prisoners were taught the code, and soon elaborate games and formal "lectures" were organized to keep their minds occupied. Phil says the most damaging part of being a POW was the isolation. If it hadn't been for the mutual support through the communication system they devised, few would have survived the torture and horrible conditions. The strong personal relationships that he developed supported him through eight years of imprisonment.

Phil feels the men owed their courage and tremendous endurance to their refusal to lose their optimism, and that humor was an essential factor. He told me a story about Skip, a pilot from his squadron who was shot down eight months after he was. After being blindfolded, bound with ropes, and tortured for weeks in an unsuccessful effort to get a tape-recorded "confession," Skip was finally moved to the cell next to Phil's. The first message Skip tapped through the wall was, "Sorry I didn't get over to you sooner, Phil, but I've been all tied up with other things." The POW's were strengthened and unified by such humor.

Phil still maintains this ability to put things in perspective. When he was shot down, he was declared "Killed in Action," and there were three memorial services held for him: one in his hometown, one at his base in California, and one on the ship. He says, with a slight grin, "I have some terrific news clippings in my scrapbook."

Optimism was actually enforced among the POW's because pessimism is so demoralizing. The men realized they couldn't afford the luxury of constant pessimistic grumblings, because both pessimism and optimism become self-fulfilling prophecies. "We had to remain optimistic to survive," Phil says. He calls optimism and humor the "glue and grease of life. Optimism is like glue because it unites us with people as we work together to accomplish our goals and objectives. Humor greases up the tough times so we can slide through being tired, sick, disappointed, depressed, bored, or even growing old. People who share a strong sense of optimistic purpose are absolutely unstoppable."

Optimism + humor = resilience—that's Phil Butler's formula.

After his repatriation, Phil was awarded two Silver Stars, the Legion of Merit, Bronze Stars, and Purple Hearts for heroism, but he didn't stop there. He went on to earn a Ph.D. in sociology and completed a successful Navy career. Now he's one of the top speakers and consultants in the country. He's living proof that our true prison is negative thoughts. Resilient thinking is the key to unlocking the door.

RESILIENCE BUILDER

Resilient Thinking

Like most athletes, I've found that the true benefit of exercise comes at the end. That's when you discover new endurance and stamina. As you stretch your muscles, some fibers rupture and the nerves may register pain, but within forty-eight hours, nature compensates and the muscle fiber is stronger than before.

Attitudes work the same way. When you stretch your resiliency just slightly beyond its current limits, your emotional fiber is stretched. Then nature compensates, and the next time that fiber is stronger. Here are eight strategies and exercises to improve your attitude fitness.

1. Catch Some Optimism

Remember that attitudes are contagious, so join a Mental Health Club by identifying the optimistic people in your life. Pessimistic people will always be a part of our lives. We can't control other people's attitudes, but we can control which people we choose to spend leisure time with. Resilient people build a supportive two-way network of friends who share each other's problems, triumphs, hopes, and possibilities.

2. Challenge Your Pessimistic Beliefs

What evidence do you have to support a doom-and-gloom attitude? If you have insufficient evidence for pessimistic views, why not abandon them? If you have ample evidence that the bad stuff is real, why not choose to redefine it in a positive way? Accept that some things in life will always be beyond our control. The only thing we can be sure of changing is our own attitude.

3. Challenge Your Irrational Beliefs

Have you convinced yourself that the following statements are true?

- I must be loved and respected by all.
- I must be completely happy all the time.
- I must be the best at everything I attempt.

These irrational beliefs lead to anxiety and pessimism. Give yourself permission to have occasional "down" days and failures. Paradoxically, this will increase your resilience.

4. Evaluate Your Positive Beliefs

- When confronted with challenges, do I view them as potential opportunities rather than insurmountable problems?
- Do I expect the best for myself and others?
- Do I try to distinguish between what I can and can't control?
- Do I expect things to work out well?

If you can answer "yes" or "almost always" to these questions, you've acquired the first key to resilience.

5. Make a Priority List

If the prospect of being optimistic in every facet of your life is overwhelming, identify one area that would benefit from improved attitude habits—career, relationships, or health, for example. By focusing on what is most important to you, you'll notice results sooner and fuel yourself to tackle your attitude toward other parts of your life.

6. Focus on What Needs to Be Done

Resilient people concentrate on what will solve the problem. Pessimists, when faced with difficulties, often turn their attention inward: "Why me? Why now? I'm incapable and overwhelmed." If you're tempted by pessimistic thoughts, ask yourself these questions.

- What is the worst possible outcome? (Let your imagination run wild.)
- Could I live with it? (Run a mental movie of how you would act and feel. You'll probably discover that you'd be able to handle it.)
- What is the likelihood this will happen? (If you were Lloyds of London, what odds would you give? Ten to one? Four hundred thousand to one? Realistically, would you be willing to gamble that it *will* happen?)
- What can I do to ensure a positive outcome? (Here's where your vivid imagination can be put to positive use. Make a list of at least three things a sensible person would do.)

Then concentrate on controlling what you can control, confident of a positive outcome but prepared to accept a negative one because you've done your best. Unresilient people think in terms of problems. Resilient people think in terms of solutions.

And, no matter what anyone else tells you, the most important messages you get every day are those you send yourself. Make them resilient! When you feel trapped in a negative state, stop and ASK yourself:

- Is my self-talk **A** - accurate?
    S - supportive?
    K - kind?

Soufflé

One of my earliest role models for resilience had stubby, hairy legs, lopsided ears, and eyes of two different colors. In fact, she was the homeliest dog in the neighborhood. That's why we gave her a very elegant name: Soufflé. Whenever I feel my resilience start to slip, I think of Soufflé and her incredible persistence and bounce. Day or night, rain or shine, whenever the Crawford doorbell rang, Soufflé was always the first one at the door. And do you know what? In fourteen years, it was never for her. That's resilience.

2

Flex Your Humor Muscles

SHRINK MOUNTAINS INTO MOLEHILLS

Fifteen thousand people still remember a charming, unintentional double entendre my wife, Donna, made. I was the closing speaker at the National Amway Free Enterprise Day in Ogden, Utah, sharing the platform with Les Brown, Dr. Joyce Brothers, and Oliver North. (I was the only person on that platform that I'd never heard of!) After my presentation, the master of ceremonies, Dexter Yager, saw Donna in the audience and urged her to come up and "say a few words." She thanked everyone for their tremendous hospitality and then described briefly how we had met and fallen in love. She concluded, "Even though Roger is missing seven fingers and one leg, he's still the most fully equipped man I've ever met." Donna stopped suddenly, realizing what she had said, and there was dead silence. But instead of freezing up, Donna burst out laughing, and the audience laughed with her for five full minutes. To this day, when we run into anyone who attended that convention, the first thing they mention is Donna's impromptu remark.

Go for the Bounce

Flexibility—bounce, spring, responsiveness—is essential for personal and business success. This may surprise you because the popular image of strong, successful people is that they *aren't* flexible, that they have the courage of their convictions so they dig in their heels and refuse to budge when challenged. They don't waffle or change their minds, and their upper lips are permanently stiff. There is a certain comforting grandeur in this image of a rocklike individual resisting a volatile world. But it's a question of knowing when to hold 'em and when to fold 'em.

Resilient, highly flexible people can explore and select from a wide variety of approaches to problems without losing sight of the overall goal. They are loose enough to wait to see the whole picture, rather than rushing to come up with premature (and possibly flawed) solutions. In contrast, inflexible, unresilient people have very little openness to the new or unexpected. They're less able to adapt and adjust, and they're reluctant to think or to do things differently.

Flexibility is essential for resourceful problem solving. You know where you're coming from and the general direction you're going, but you're flexible about how you get there. You can find new approaches, work around problems, uncover innovative solutions, and develop unique plans. When one approach fails, you try something else. But when you're convinced there's only one way to tackle a problem, you're risking discouragement and negativity if your plans don't pan out.

Rx for Flexibility: Humor

Remember prisoner of war Phil Butler's formula: optimism + humor = resilience? If the first step to resilience is to believe success is possible, then the second step is to give yourself permission to laugh. Nothing increases our bounce factor faster than learning to use humor productively. Humor acts as a buffer against stress, an antidote to paralyzing perfectionism, and a way to widen your perspective. It wards off depression and contributes to good health. It is also essential for smoothing over frustrating or embarrassing business and personal situations, providing a glue of shared awareness.

What if Donna hadn't laughed at her slip of the tongue? What if she had turned beet-red and rushed off the platform in tears? There probably would have been a stunned and embarrassed silence, then a definite chill over the rest of the presentation. Instead, Donna created a win-win situation of shared delight.

When you're in a flexible state of mind, you see life's possibilities in amazing new ways. My friend Mike Lee is an avid baseball player, skier, diver, and golfer. One day the top golfer at his club was complaining about the lack of competition. Mike thought of a creative way to put some ice on this gentleman's swollen ego.

Mike approached the champ and suggested they play eighteen holes. He was somewhat taken aback by Mike's audacity and replied sarcastically, "It depends on your handicap." Mike suggested a small wager on the outcome. That piqued the champ's interest, and he accepted the challenge. Mike's only stipulation was that he, Mike, would select the time.

At 11:00 P.M. that night, Mike Lee beat the club champion. Mike, who is blind, played as he always does—with his guide dog at his side, in the dark.

Laughter is a powerful tool for fortifying resilience. The ability to laugh at a situation gives us a sense of control. We are less likely to feel nonresilient and helpless when we can laugh at what is challenging us. However, laughter isn't the primary reason for encouraging humor, nor is it the main way to express humor. Humor is a philosophy more than a facial expression. It's the long view, the little step back from the fray. Humor permeates every aspect of our lives and generates a core sense of well-being. It makes us confident that we'll almost always be able to respond flexibly, to "go with the flow," because, even in the midst of trials, there will be a moment or a memory that can make us smile.

Humor is, hands down, the most effective and simplest tool for dealing with tension, surprise, and inconsistency, three irritants we all encounter daily. Of course, grim fortitude and enormous strength of will can overcome them too, but humor is a heck of a lot easier and more fun. Whenever life just doesn't make sense, we can use humor to explain the gaps—or just to relieve the stress.

Everyone feels better after they laugh. That's one reason we're told so often that laughter is great medicine. A Stanford Medical School researcher found that laughing boosts the body's immune system, invigorates the white blood cells and provides more oxygen to the red cells, discourages pulmonary bacterial growth, exercises the heart and many muscle groups, raises metabolism, and increases alertness, animation, and personal interaction. In other words, humor is good for you.

I believe that we're all born with the gift of laughter, but, somewhere along the way, some of us misplace it or get it drummed out of us. You can probably remember your parents and teachers telling you, "Don't be so silly"—"Grow up"—"Act your age." The message we got was that silliness is reserved for youth, so we must become more serious and less lighthearted as we mature. We all need more silliness in our lives. That's because *silly* comes from the Old English word *selig*, which meant to be happy, blessed, healthy, and prosperous. Of course, we would never say to someone, "Stop being so happy, healthy, and prosperous." (The next time you run into someone down in the dumps, wish them "a day with much silliness" and watch their reaction.)

Lightening Up

"What pushes *your* buttons?" Oprah Winfrey asked her audience during an interview with Daniel Goleman, author of *Emotional Intelligence*. One man told Oprah about a recent visit to a giant hardware store. He approached a clerk who was wearing a brightly colored vest inscribed in big letters, Ask Me Anything.

"Where's the caulking?" the man asked.

"I don't know," replied the young clerk.

Now, you and I would probably have smiled (discreetly so as not to hurt the teenager's feelings) at the incongruity, and then gone in search of a more knowledgeable clerk. However, this man felt that the universe, in the person of this clerk, was out to get him. As he retold the story to Oprah, he relived his anger. He realized, of course, that he couldn't blame all the world's ills on one sales clerk, so he moved up the food chain: "I hold the manager responsible. He didn't train his staff. I wanted to have him *right here*!" And he demonstrated seizing an imaginary opponent by the shoulders. His face was red, his eyes were bulging, and he was clearly reliving every infuriating moment of this incident.

Oprah countered with a similar experience of her own. She was looking for a copy of one of the best-known novels of her youth, *The Catcher in the Rye*. She approached a young clerk in a large bookstore and asked, "Where is J. D. Salinger?"

"Oh, he doesn't work here," said the clerk.

Here were all the necessary ingredients of humor: surprise, irony, mistaking one thing for another, and a charming anecdote that Oprah could tell for years to come. Instead of becoming angry, Oprah laughed. Of course, there was a certain poignancy in realizing that the giants of one's youth have been replaced by new giants, but at the very least, she had the opportunity to increase the clerk's knowledge of famous authors. The book buyer and the caulk buyer were confronted with similar situations. One saw the humor. The other didn't. Which one was the winner?

Jack Canfield, a dear friend who used one of my stories in his best-seller *Chicken Soup for the Soul,* told me how a good belly laugh helped him survive a stressful situation. He was making an important speech at a hotel in Cincinnati, and had had several thousand copies of his book shipped ahead for the delegates. When he arrived, he asked for the books. No one had any idea where they were. He checked with the carrier and learned that they had been signed for by "José." Unfortunately, there were at least fifteen men named José working at that hotel.

For the next five hours, everyone searched diligently for those books. Time was getting short. Jack's good humor, blood pressure, and business reputation were all at risk. Finally, the right José was located, and he led them to where he had put the boxes. They were neatly and logically stacked in the food-storage area with the other canned soups! Rather than being furious, Jack showed his resilience by laughing long and hard at this very rational misunderstanding. (Knowing Jack, he would have found something to laugh about even if the books hadn't turned up.)

Funny Business—Humor at Work

Some of the groups I speak to are terminally adult: no laughs, no having a good time. "This is serious business" is deeply engraved on every face. I like to remind them that you can take your work seriously without taking *yourself* seriously.

BOUNCE HIGHER TIP

If you take resilience seriously,
you'll take yourself lightly.

Any workplace that values effective, flexible, and creative employees should also value the cost-free power of humor. Nothing beats a good laugh for putting difficult and complex problems in perspective. The role of laughter in relieving stress is so important that some businesses now conduct humor workshops for their employees. We all know the high costs of stress in the workplace: high turnover rates, low productivity, frequent absences due to illness and injuries, psychological problems that disrupt and even endanger other employees. Workplace humor has become imperative for surviving the turbulent times we face in the business world.

Andrew Yarborough is the manager of quality-assurance engineering for the Radius Corporation. He's also two feet tall. I met Andrew when I was taken on a tour of Radius's home office facility in Sunnyvale, California. Radius has developed some truly fascinating technology, including the software used for animation in the movie *Jurassic Park*. As I went from floor to floor, at least five people mentioned that I had to see Andrew's office before I left. Then they chuckled. I was definitely intrigued.

The quality-assurance department on the second floor has those ubiquitous, identical office cubicles. Suddenly I noticed that the doorway of one cubicle had a large rope net draped in front of it. It was the kind you'd use on a safari to capture a lion or rhino. As I got closer, I saw that the net stopped about thirty inches from the floor, and there was a sign next to it: Tall People Filter. This had to be Andrew's office.

Andrew Yarborough was born with a bone disease that limited his growth. Few things in our world are geared to people two feet high, so he designed this humorous way to give the rest of us some perspective on encountering physical obstacles. In his own work space, Andrew can enter easily, while we tall folks have to duck. His sense of humor helped to break down any preconceptions of fellow employees while stimulating a sense of lightheartedness and camaraderie. Andrew Yarborough understands that laughter and having fun in a business environment are not unprofessional.

After observing many top CEO's during the last decade, I'm convinced that the most effective managers and leaders are the ones who model and encourage humor on the job. They understand that laughter can keep us healthier, more productive, and better able to influence others. Of course, some people can reach the top in their field without possessing the tiniest trace of humor, but your ascent will be more fun, rewarding, and healthful if you use humor. And you'll see a lot of smiling faces along the way.

Childish Laughter

When was the last time you really laughed? Many adults have been taught that laughter isn't quite polite. Some even cover their mouths when they laugh, ashamed of any lightheartedness. Children, however, have a great sense of joy, wonderment, serenity, and laughter.

Recently my daughter, Alexa, and I were out for a walk and we came upon our neighbor's dachshund. This dog loves to chase its tail, and there it was, circling faster and faster. This really tickled Alexa, and she laughed until she ended up rolling around on the ground. Can you remember the last time you laughed so hard that your legs went out from under you? Wouldn't it feel wonderful to experience that much joy?

Resilient people have taught themselves to see and enjoy everyday life with the excited eyes of a child. I thought I had this skill already, but having a child of my own has really reminded me of life's endless possibilities. When Alexa was two, we were in Hawaii during a rainstorm. Afterward, a big rainbow lit up the sky. I explained what a rainbow was and she kept staring at it, completely fascinated, until it was gone. Back home in California on a gray and gloomy day, it started to rain just as we were going out. I told Alexa to go get her raincoat, but she corrected me. "No, Daddy, that's my *rainbow coat*."

Cost-Free and Irresistible

Even when you don't feel like laughing, try smiling. That smiling draws positive attention to you and tends to make you and others feel at ease. Smiling conveys self-acceptance and an accepting attitude toward others. It increases others' confidence in themselves and in you. Smiling makes you appear approachable, friendly, relaxed, open, and comfortable.

How can you smile when you're having a really difficult day that is testing your resilience to the max? My method is to search my mind for one bright spot, pleasant thought, or hidden blessing and then to concentrate on it. As soon as I can find a smile, it helps me relax and stay positive.

A smile is such a simple thing, but it starts a whole sequence of physical and psychological responses. It reduces muscular tension in the face. (You can't contract your forehead into painful wrinkles when you're smiling.) It connects us with our positive life experiences, illuminating the dark places and putting difficulties in perspective.

Some people remain skeptical when I plug the value of a smile. It just can't be that simple, they think. One was a young woman who told me she was "just a food server." On a typical day, she would arrive early, help cook the food, and then ladle it onto plates as people filed past. "Each line in our cafeteria serves an identical meal. I'm not sure how your attitude thing is going to make any difference, but I'm willing to try it." A few months later I heard from her again. She told me she had decided to greet all the people in her line with a smile when she handed them their plates. The results were dramatic, but now she had a problem: "Everyone lines up in my line and it creates a bottleneck."

I've learned that I can't control people's reactions to me, but I *can* control how I respond to them. When I'm open and friendly, most people are open and friendly back. When I give people a warm, friendly smile, the amazing thing is that I almost always get a warm, friendly smile back.

Laughter, the Lifeline

Look! Up in the sky! Cinema's most recent Superman, Christopher Reeve, was the ultimate personification of the invincible

Man of Steel. So it was doubly shocking when the forty-two-year-old actor broke his neck and was paralyzed from the neck down in a 1995 riding accident. For weeks, Reeve lay heavily sedated, fading in and out of consciousness. No one was sure if he'd live, much less ever be able to breathe on his own or move his arms and legs. One day, Reeve looked up to find an outrageously eccentric doctor in a surgical mask hovering over him. Suddenly he realized that the "doctor" was his acting-school buddy, comedian Robin Williams. For the first time since the accident, Reeve laughed. "At that moment, I knew that life could be good again," he said.

Reeve told interviewer Barbara Walters about his hopes and plans for the future. Of course, there were times when he was discouraged and felt like giving up, but he drew on the support of his family and his own reservoir of resilience. And laughter. "Robin knew that my first laugh would be the hardest, but it would be my first step towards healing," said Reeve. Still dependent on a ventilator to breathe, Reeve talked about directing a film and even acting as soon as he was able to sit up in a wheelchair. Two years later he did!

BOUNCE HIGHER TIP

*Humor is a powerful analgesic.
It's free, nonprescription, has no side effects,
and is completely habit-forming.*

Contagious laughter is a powerful antidote for pain and fear. A young soldier in the D day invasion of Normandy described the dark hours crossing the English Channel in a landing barge before reaching the beaches of Normandy. "[We were] scared silly," he recalled. "I don't know who started to laugh, but soon we were all joining in hilarious laughter . . . laughing our heads off . . . the fright that had possessed us was soon replaced by a wonderful feeling. Had Hitler seen us laughing, he would have thrown in the towel then and there."

Beating Deadly Perfectionism

Individuals who struggle with resilience often struggle with perfectionism. Nothing can ever be perfect, so a continuous quest for perfection in ourselves and others is futile. The irony for perfectionists is that no matter how successful they may be, they will inevitably find a flaw that wipes out all their satisfaction and sense of accomplishment.

Unrealistic, rigid perfectionism jeopardizes resilience. We all strive to excel, but unrealistic standards can actually keep us from doing and being our best. People who seek strength by adopting impossible standards and role models reduce their resilience. Currently, there is an epidemic of potentially lethal eating disorders among young women and steroid use among young men. They're destroying themselves in the quest to become "perfect," which they translate as looking like the ideals promoted by the popular media—impossibly skeletal fashion models and improbably muscled athletes.

Even well-adjusted adults can fall into the perfectionism trap, succumbing to procrastination and paralysis because they fear that perfection is unlikely. What was the last challenge you declined because the possibility of failure made you too uncomfortable? Was it perhaps worth a try anyway? Remember the saying, Anything worth doing is worth doing badly . . . at first.

BOUNCE HIGHER TIP

*Notice what you've already accomplished,
not just what you still have to do.*

Has your striving for excellence slid over the line into debilitating perfectionism? Take this simple quiz to find out.

1. Is the pleasure of your accomplishments often dimmed because you think you should have done better?

2. Are you frequently anxious or angry because others don't meet your standards?

3. Are you uncomfortable when you can't control your surroundings?

4. Do you ever skip doing something because you might not do it as well as you should?

5. Do your high standards sometimes lead to procrastination, paralysis, or apathy?

6. Do you feel you have to do everything yourself or it won't be done right?

If this describes you, then you are handicapping yourself with perfectionism.

Fortunately, perfectionism has a universal antidote: humor. Humor cuts us loose from preconceptions, making us lighter, more fluid, and better able to see the big picture. Humor helps us notice the limitations of our search for perfection, so we can actually accomplish more and do better. Humor is expansive rather than restrictive.

A delightful acquaintance named Norma Isaacs told me how her children cured her of her perfectionism. She was expecting important guests, the kind for which the house is not only cleaned but also redecorated. As part of her preparations, Norma had purchased brand-new living-room furniture, and had the older pieces slipcovered and moved to the family room. On the big day, Norma's husband came to pick her up after work, notably nervous. "What's wrong?" she demanded. He assured her that everyone was alive and well and the house was still standing. "What's wrong?" she repeated, relieved but feeling a sense of rising panic. He refused to tell her and they drove home in silence.

When she entered the house, her children were waiting to greet her, looking distinctly uncomfortable. She walked into the family room and let out a shriek. The slipcovered sofa now resembled not so much a place to sit as a piece of abstract sculpture. What had happened was this: One of the children had accidentally spilled something on the new slipcovers. Norma's ten-year-old daughter was an enterprising child. Knowing what a perfectionist her mother was, she had resolved to solve the problem before Mommy got home. She stripped off the slipcovers and washed them in the washing machine. The covers shrank. No amount of pushing would get the ample cushions back into them. Since the covers were too small for the cushions, the logical thing to do was reduce the size of the cushions. The child got a sharp knife and sawed a few inches off each cushion, forced them into the covers, and zipped the zippers. Now the cushions lay, like twisted biscuits, on a misshapen hulk of upholstery straining inside a corset of shrunken slipcover.

Norma stood and surveyed the results of her daughter's hard work. Suddenly, she realized that if she hadn't had such a reputation for perfectionism, the original spot would have been left for her to handle at her leisure after the guests had departed. She began to chuckle at the absurdity of the couch and the absurdity of her everything-must-always-be-perfect attitude. She had four helpful, healthy children, a patient husband, and a house that hadn't burned down. "That's enough for anyone!" Norma says. "My family finally cured me of my perfectionism by showing me what's important in life."

Surfing the Waves of Change

People have a love/hate relationship with change. We love the opportunities for growth and expanding our horizons, but we hate the uncertainty of change, the feeling that we are no longer in control. We can get excited about a new home, a new relationship, visiting a new place, or mastering new technology, but we also fear loss of security and identity. It is unsettling to think that our job might not be there tomorrow, or that our economic security might be threatened. However, people who actively maintain an attitude of flexibility have a powerful buffer against the inevitable stresses and strains of change.

BOUNCE HIGHER TIP

*Life's inevitable changes are like
a compulsory roller-coaster ride.
You can cower and shut your eyes tight,
or you can exult in the thrills.*

Ron Areglado, vice president of the National Association of Elementary School Principals, told me about an Illinois school district that had suffered severe budget cuts. Morale was at an all-time low. A school bond issue had been placed before the voters and failed miserably. Many teachers had to be laid off, and now the district superintendent faced the first teachers' in-service day of the fall term. He would have to tell the staff-cut survivors about even more changes ahead in scheduling and class size. This hardly seemed an occasion for humor.

On in-service day, the remaining teachers and staff straggled into the auditorium, clearly dispirited. Many were suffering from "survivor's guilt," upset by the absence of their former colleagues. But when they saw the district superintendent walk in, they gaped in astonishment. The usually dignified man was wearing a long pink gown and sequined shoes.

The superintendent went backstage, the auditorium lights dimmed, and the curtain rose on a scene from *Cinderella*. The superintendent, portraying one of the ugly stepsisters, struggled to force his size-12 foot into Cinderella's tiny slipper. "Keep trying! I know it will fit!" he shouted in a falsetto voice.

When all attempts had failed, the ugly stepsister turned to the audience and said in his normal voice, "Because of the many changes we're facing in this district, we all feel a little like Cinderella's stepsisters—*too much foot and not enough shoe!*"

The audience loved it and he received a standing ovation. The superintendent had responded playfully to a difficult situation, acknowledging his staff's pain and then gently directing their attention to the many changes and challenges they would be discussing that day. As a leader, he realized that an organization cannot simultaneously mourn the past and move to a new future. First, he had to help them let go of the past, and he chose humor as his tool. Beginning the school year by laughing together would be a strong foundation to build on.

Shared laughter can be the first step to accepting change. It doesn't deny pain or minimize challenges, but it helps people tap into their reservoirs of positive feelings. During times of change, these positive feelings can reenergize us and strengthen our resilience.

P R O F I L E
Julia Sweeney

Often we count on the funny people of the world to lighten our daily load, but what happens when a professional humorist's life turns upside down?

Comedian Julia Sweeney turned a family tragedy into a triumph of understanding and insight by celebrating the humor in life.

Julia's list of stage, screen, and TV credits includes four years on *Saturday Night Live,* which featured her hilariously androgynous character "Pat." In 1995, she had just bought her first house, a small tree-shaded bungalow in Hollywood, and she was adjusting to living alone following a divorce. Disney was about to release a feature film built around her "Pat" character. Her career was booming, and she was looking forward to "living gloriously alone" in her private Shangri-la with her three cats.

Then she got the call. Her beloved brother Mike had stage-4 lymphoma. ("There are only four stages.") The doctors gave him a 40-percent chance of recovery. Using resilient thinking, Julia decided it was "like a class where you had to be in the top 40 percent to graduate. Easy."

A week later, the "Pat" movie opened to disastrous reviews and sank instantly into oblivion. However, this career setback seemed irrelevant beside the intense human struggle that had engulfed her life.

Mike came to stay with Julia while undergoing painful chemotherapy and radiation therapy at a nearby medical center. In her wise and funny book, *God Said "Ha!,"* she recalls how they named her Shangri-la "the International House of Cancer." They dubbed Mike's debilitating chemotherapy cocktail "Drano" and the equipment-filled radiation room "the starship *Enterprise*." In the long, tedious hours in hospital waiting rooms, they found ways to keep smiling. Mike decided that his sister's reward for these endless hospital visits should be a "fabulous doctor husband," so they covertly rated the cuteness of each passing physician in the hallway. If one of Mike's doctors turned out to be married, Mike would playfully ask for a second opinion.

Humor eased Mike's pain and lifted his spirits, but he continued to decline. It seemed inconceivable that life could become any more intense. Then incredibly, following a routine checkup, Julia learned she also had cancer—a rare but curable type of cervical cancer that had spread to her uterus and fallopian tubes. A hysterectomy would save her life but end her long-cherished plans for motherhood.

Her family was shocked and devastated, but Mike immediately saw the irony of it. "You just couldn't stand it, you being an actress and me getting all the spotlight," he joked. They called it her "sympathy cancer." Julia decided that if you have to get cancer, the reproductive organs are the place to do it because they're easier to live without than your liver or lungs. "This led me to thinking," Julia comments. "What if you got cancer of the fat? You'd have to have emergency liposuction."

Before Julia's surgery, Mike worsened. He had loved boats and the ocean, so his friends gently rocked his mattress and dipped his hands in buckets of water. "Mike," they murmured, "you're in a boat. We're ferrying you." And that's how Mike died, ferried across an "ocean" by those who loved him.

Julia had been so involved in Mike's illness that she hadn't given much thought to her own cancer. Three days after Mike's death, she had a hysterectomy. "I spent plenty of moments in anguish, coming to terms with my reality, but sometimes it's in your limitations that you find your greatest strengths."

Julia has bounced back from this difficult and painful experience. She turned her real-life story into a one-woman Broadway show, which got rave reviews. She sent a clear and powerful message to the audience that they too could persevere as long as they stayed tuned to the genuine humor that life presents. "Life," Julia says, "isn't too bad if you can pull off a little attitude adjustment."

RESILIENCE BUILDER

Flex Your Humor Muscles

Flexible people don't get locked into just one way of thinking. They can shift perspective and reappraise difficult or threatening situations.

1. What Pushes Your Buttons?

What kinds of situations are most likely to derail you or keep you from doing and feeling your best? Make a list of what can get you down or any major changes you are going through. Then decide which humor strategies will be most effective in each situation:

- focusing on the incongruity
- savoring the irony
- satirizing the situation
- mentally scripting the event into a humorous anecdote you can retell

See yourself responding flexibly, using humor in positive ways. Mentally rehearse your new reactions until they come naturally.

2. What Pushes Other People's Buttons?

Think of some people you'd like to have greater rapport with. Would building a bridge of shared humor and laughter be an effective tool to achieve this? Is there someone close to you who is suffering from physical pain, excessive stress, or crippling perfectionism? Are you in a position to offer them new insights and attitudes incorporating humor? If so, what strategies could you try?

3. Three Quick Pick-Me-Ups

- Go to a silly movie and watch it with the eyes of a child. Better yet, watch it *with* a child.
- Think about the last time you had a real belly laugh. What triggered it? How did it make you feel? Can you repeat the experience?
- Recall a couple of jokes you thought were hilarious in sixth grade. See if you can get some coworkers to share theirs.

A Funny Ending

Airports are great places for people watching. Whenever I'm between planes, I try to find time to observe my fellow humans. One summer day I approached the only empty seat in the waiting area and found that someone had left a newspaper on it. My hands were full of luggage so I sat down right on top of it. Since it was a hot day, I was wearing shorts and a short-sleeved shirt.

A man was sitting across from me approximately ten feet away. He immediately noticed my artificial leg and, a few moments later, my hands. He looked as though he was desperately trying to conceal his curiosity. I could tell he was staring at me, because whenever our eyes would meet he would quickly glance at the floor or up to the ceiling. After a few minutes, he walked over to me. I anticipated he was going to ask me one of the questions that I've heard many times in the past: "Sir, were you born this way?" or "Were you in an accident?" But I was wrong.

"Excuse me, sir," he said. "I'm sorry to bother you, but have you finished reading that newspaper?"

I thought to myself, what *kind* of physical challenge does he think I have? "I'm not quite finished." I said. I got up, turned the page, and sat down again. We both burst out laughing. Shared laughter is one of life's great pleasures.

3

Bank on Your Past

OPEN A
RESILIENCE ACCOUNT

"Get your kicks on Route 66." A recording of that bouncy old song was playing in the airport when I arrived, and in my mind I ticked off the cities along the route in time with the music: St. Louis—Joplin—"Oklahoma City is mighty pretty."

The poignancy hit home. I've been to Oklahoma City many times, but this was my first visit there after the 1995 terrorist bombing. I can think of few people who have had to discover more inner resources than the citizens of Oklahoma City.

That evening, I glanced out my hotel-room window and saw in the distance the bleak, rubble-strewn lot that was once the nine-story Murrah Federal Building. The fence around it was still dotted with tattered squares of paper and bunches of flowers, a spontaneous shrine to the 169 adults and children known to have lost their lives there. A few days after the devastating explosion, I had phoned the organization that invited me to speak, the Oklahoma State School Boards Association. "Is it appropriate if I talk about the bombing?" I asked. Their reply assured me: "I think we're more eager now than ever to hear your message."

Later that evening, I went for a walk that took me past many damaged buildings and, inevitably, to that fence. The site was much larger than I had expected, eerily quiet and dark in the heart of the city. Up close, I could see the photos tacked to the fence, dozens of smiling faces. Most had messages written on them. Some photos were of children my daughter's age. I thought of what their parents must be enduring, and suddenly tears welled up in my eyes. Television, despite its immediacy, can never convey the enormity of a disaster like this.

As I walked back to the hotel, I pondered what I could possibly say to these people who had gone through so much. Were there any words that could begin to touch their grief? Even if they hadn't lost someone they knew and loved, everyone in that audience, like everyone in Oklahoma City, had experienced a profound loss.

The next day, I stood on the stage of the Myriad Convention Center, on the same spot where President Clinton had spoken during the memorial service. There are many ways to try to explain a tragedy, but I didn't attempt it. Instead, I told this audience about the ways they had inspired the world.

I talked about the conversations I had just had with several Oklahomans. One was George Morrison, the legendary silver-haired bellman who had served at the Skurvin Hotel for forty years until it closed, and now presided at the Medallion Hotel. He was on the job that morning when the bomb went off six blocks away. The ground heaved and George dashed out into the street, sure that it was an earthquake. A few moments later, he saw people running toward him, bleeding, blackened by smoke, and covered with shards of broken glass.

Many would have been too stunned to do more than gape, but George immediately went into action. He directed the victims into the hotel lobby, where he administered first aid as best he could.

Many of the injured, he told me, set to work comforting those more seriously hurt, getting them water, blankets, and sugar-rich drinks to prevent shock. People with deep cuts were ignoring their wounds and carrying others in their arms. George also found it significant that race, age, and economic status no longer mattered. Everyone there was determined to help everyone else.

In the past, George said, some people thought of their city as just an overgrown small town. If anyone had asked them whether the city had enough resources to handle a major disaster, most would have replied, "Absolutely not." But the city came through. People did more than they ever imagined they could, and the resulting sense of unity created bonds that will never be broken. We don't realize how resilient we can be until we are tested.

I told them how the world had been moved by the bravery of the gallant rescue worker Rebecca Anderson, killed by falling wreckage as she struggled to save others. And I talked about the young woman Daina Bradley, who was trapped under a huge slab of concrete for several days. To free her, rescuers had to amputate one of her legs as the surrounding debris threatened to crush them all. Later, she learned that her mother and her two children had died in the explosion.

The audience positively lit up when I mentioned her. After my talk, they gathered around me to ask if I'd seen Daina take her first step with her new leg. I hadn't, and they eagerly and proudly described it. The occasion had received national TV coverage. As a city held its breath, this smiling survivor stood up and walked. Despite everything that had happened, there she was, still standing tall. It was an electrifying and symbolic moment for every Oklahoman, proof that the healing had begun. One man said, "When Daina Bradley, who had lost so much, had enough courage to stand on her artificial leg and take her first step and do that with a smile, that's when I realized that we all could recover." By celebrating this victory, they added to their stockpile of resilience for coping with future challenges.

One of the association members told me that being from Oklahoma will never be the same again. "We're proud of how we handled this tremendous adversity. We had to reinvent who we are and how we view ourselves as people in our state. We've had to find the positive in this turmoil and we've done it."

What I learned from the people of Oklahoma City: *Challenges are inevitable; defeat is optional.*

The Past as Fuel for the Future

Your ability to tap your past for strength and inspiration—to build on your past—is a critical key to your future resilience. If you define your life as a history of overcoming obstacles, solving problems, and achieving goals, you are recognizing your fortitude to continue. Using your past doesn't mean rewriting history. It's just adopting an optimistic attitude-filter.

Resilient people can view the events of their pasts, positive or negative, as valuable lessons in competency and control. Unresilient people may look at similar events and see images of inadequacy and failure. Then they try to protect themselves by blocking the past and focusing only on the future ("Today is the first day of the rest of my life").

But past experiences aren't just a bonus for resilience, they're a requisite. Resilient individuals and organizations filter their past experiences, good and bad, to extract strength, inspiration, and wisdom. For example, the people of Oklahoma City will always be able to draw on their memories of survival, no matter what they may face in the future. You too can decide to use your past as fuel for your future.

Building Block #1—Your Past Successes

If you are going to stay resilient, you need to feel that a specific action will produce a specific result. Sounds simple—yet how many people really make the connection?

The more you think that the positive things in your life are the result of your own efforts, the more likely you are to believe that future achievement is possible. When you identify a cause-and-effect pattern, you feel competent and confident.

But if you see success as largely a matter of luck or coincidence, then it is going to seem beyond your control. There is little you can actively do to achieve it, and even if it does come your way, it can be snatched from you at any time.

One key to resilient thinking is to focus on the *process* of the achievement, not just on the goal. Notice how your efforts helped produce the results you wanted, step by step. The process reaffirms our resilience and gives us the confidence to keep trying, even if we temporarily fall short of our goal. We still have proof that our past accomplishment wasn't just luck or chance. We possess whatever is needed to succeed. We did it before; we can do it again.

Process is more important than product. If you doubt this, ask yourself if winning or inheriting a million dollars would increase your confidence in your personal resilience and resources. Many inheritors of great fortunes have been noted for their unhappiness and sense of futility. Many past jackpot winners rate themselves worse off than before. The happy ones are those who already believed in their own mental and spiritual wealth and their ability to cope and achieve before their unexpected financial bonanza.

BOUNCE HIGHER TIP

Focus on process, not product.

There was a young man—I'll call him Steve—in the audience when I addressed a group of salespeople at John Hancock Insurance in Boston. These were all newer employees indentified as having great potential, and my topic was "Creating the Champion Within." One of my key ideas was that you can't survive the daily rejections salespeople face unless you develop what I call *internal boldness.* You do this by focusing on and celebrating the past successes in your life.

Steve stopped to talk to me after my presentation. He was intellectually convinced by my viewpoint, he told me, but he still had a hard time seeing himself as an achiever. As we chatted, I learned that Steve was well educated and had won his sales position over many competitors. Still, if you don't really see yourself as an achiever, it's impossible to develop the resilience essential for achievement. You create a self-fulfilling prophecy.

Steve wasn't the first person to share such insecurities with me. Usually I start by asking, "Tell me where you're coming from." From what accomplishments can you draw strength and inspiration? Steve struggled to answer me, but every time he cited an achievement, he then dismissed or belittled it. He saw each success as a result of luck or coincidence rather than his own efforts.

Nearby, another young agent seemed to be eavesdropping. He turned out to be Steve's longtime friend. When he saw Steve's discomfort, he stepped over and put his arm around Steve's shoulders: "But Steve, you've always been someone I really admired." Steve immediately glanced down at his shoes. Clearly, he was having difficulty accepting a compliment—a characteristic of people with low resilience. I turned to Steve's friend: "Why don't you tell me where he's coming from?"

The friend laughed. "I'll never forget the time he went bungee jumping." Bungee jumping! Now, I consider myself rather adventurous, someone who thrives on testing my physical limits, but bungee jumping, especially with the elastic cord tied to my artificial leg, isn't something I've yearned to do. (I can imagine the exciting moment of rebound, my leg soaring gracefully upward, the rest of me still plummeting downward.)

He told how he and Steve had been out for a day in the park with a group of friends and had come across a giant bungee-jumping platform. No one in Steve's group was willing to try it, but Steve—this same young man who was unsure of his own boldness—immediately volunteered. He climbed the seventy-five-odd steps to the top, had the bungee cord secured to his ankles, then dove off headfirst with a boisterous, triumphant yell. And he went back four more times! Everyone was impressed by his daring.

As Steve's friend told me this story, Steve started to stand differently. This young man who had been struggling to answer the question *"Where are you coming from?"* actually assumed a different posture before our eyes. Until then, he had never thought of his daring leaps as an accomplishment. It took his friend to make him see that, yes indeed, he had exhibited courage. He had had boldness within him, and he clearly had the resilience to dare and to take a calculated risk. He just needed someone to point this out to him.

Building Block #2—Your Past Mistakes

If you want to be resilient, get on friendly terms with your mistakes. Remember that most major scientific discoveries started with a "mistake." Henry Ford said, "Even a mistake may turn out to be the one thing necessary to a worthwhile achievement." Great literature, art, and music depend on "fine surprises" (which often started as mistakes) for their power.

Whenever you try to second-guess every move you make, you're trapped in an infinite "What if?" spiral. *If you're not making mistakes, you're not moving forward.* Rather than spending your life trying to make right decisions, concentrate on making decisions right.

The benefit of mistakes (or what we decide at the time are mistakes) is that they can teach us the effect of our actions. Then we decide whether the same action might have different results in the future, or if we should try something else. Sometimes we get so caught up by our emotional response to the "mistake"—and how it is perceived by others—that we fail to step back and think it through. We're too busy beating up on ourselves to learn the lesson we've already paid for!

There are "smart" mistakes and "foolish" mistakes. The "foolish" ones are when you do the same thing over and over, despite ample evidence that your action isn't going to achieve the result you want. Smart mistakes, on the other hand, offer tremendous potential. The secret is to draw a wise conclusion from a foolish choice. The student who flunks an exam has a choice of responses.

- I'm no good at math and never will be. (**Nonresilient thinking**)
- Math is hard for me, so I need to study more if I want to pass. Maybe I can get a tutor. (**Resilient thinking**)

Which student is more likely to pass math in the future?

"I wish I had made more mistakes" is a complaint I often hear. "The biggest mistake in my life," people tell me, "was playing it safe." In retrospect, they realize they should have spent more time taking chances, making mistakes, and learning from them.

Watch children learning to walk. They will quickly convince you that everyone enters this world with a strong sense of resilience. They pull themselves up on a table or chair, take one unsteady step, and then tumble to the floor. Sometimes they bump their heads and cry for a few moments, but then they try again as if nothing had happened. Gradually, they eliminate what doesn't work and discover what does. They don't decide that they've made a mistake so they'd better stop trying. They keep going until they succeed.

A good way to judge people's level of resilience is how they respond to mistakes. Are they immediately defensive or antagonistic? Do they blame others? Or do they accept responsibility and keep going? Do mistakes make them give up? Or do they try harder? Are they afflicted with a level of perfectionism that keeps them from achieving and enjoying their achievements? People who lack resilience are usually humiliated by any perceived error. They make self-disparaging remarks, silently and even out loud: "Trust me to blow it!" "Can't take me anywhere." This may seem a harmless way to relieve frustration, even an appropriate expression of modesty. It's not. It's a sign of unresilience. No outside praise can drown out the voices we hear in our own heads and hearts.

The next time you catch yourself indulging in unresilient self-talk over a mistake, choose a mental catchphrase to get you back on track. It can be something like "Smart people make smart mistakes." Think of the tennis player who wants to recover from a poorly executed point. Cursing the ball, raging at the racket, and insulting the umpire isn't going to do it. The resilient player has developed internal self-talk to refocus on the task at hand.

We all need permission—even more from ourselves than from others—to make mistakes frequently and productively. Often, we learn more from our setbacks than from our successes. It can be more important to know how *not* to do something than how to do it. Otherwise, you'll keep on getting what you're getting as long as you keep on doing what you're doing. *Let your past instruct you.*

> ### BOUNCE HIGHER TIP
> *If you're not making mistakes, you're not learning and growing.*

Building Block #3—Your Past Adversities

We're often told to put tragedies and hard times behind us so we can get on with our lives. "Just forget about it," people say. However, I believe we should remember these experiences, retaining what can empower and enhance us. Viewed with a resilient attitude, past adversities have the potential to strengthen our ability to shape the future.

Lisa Durham was a corporate controller for a major New York publisher when she was terribly injured by a coworker. One day a disturbed employee, just fired for incompetence, sprang from hiding to attack her. Luckily, Lisa saw something coming from the corner of her eye and started to turn her head. It saved her life. Instead of hitting the back of her neck, his black-belt karate chop landed on her jaw, breaking it in three places and knocking out several teeth.

Lisa experienced the classic list of a trauma survivor's symptoms. First, there was continuing pain and the inability to eat solid food for many months. Then there was the series of reconstructive surgeries that exhausted her insurance and required her to declare bankruptcy. She lost a job she loved because she couldn't bring herself to go back to the scene of the assault. Her office, which had once seemed so secure, now loomed as a "house of horrors" in her frequent nightmares. She also experienced panic attacks, irrational fears, and depression, all typical symptoms of post-traumatic stress disorder (PTSD). The justice system was another source of frustration. The assailant was given a four-year suspended sentence. Through all this, Lisa had the secret feeling common to many victims that, somehow, she must have been responsible for the attack.

Lisa had a wonderful personal support system of family and friends. Time, medical skill, and love began to heal her body and spirit, but she couldn't put the experience behind her. Random violence can really make us feel helpless, as if we've lost control of our lives and our ability to influence our future. Lisa decided she needed to address her experience in a positive, active way before she could fully recover. She regained her sense of control by learning more about workplace assaults and about others who had had similar experiences. Lisa began researching violence in the workplace and found it was a much bigger problem than most of us imagine.

She became an active member of several victims'-rights groups, including Justice for All and the Victims of Crime Advocacy League (VOCAL), supporting legislation for victims' rights and stiffer sentences. Her focus has expanded to all victims of violent crime, and she is working with the New York State District Attorney's office to establish an 800 number that will provide counseling and support to victims and their families. "I took a negative experience in my life," she says, "and turned it into a positive one. . . . For me, this [work] has been an educational experience, and instrumental in my recovery. Being an advocate is not for everyone, but it worked for me."

Countries and cultures have always relied on their histories to instruct and inspire new generations. But how many of today's organizations draw on their past to survive and prosper in challenging times? Once I attended a company meeting where everyone was about as dispirited as you can get. The company was having financial difficulties, and the morale seemed slightly lower than a snail's eyebrow. Then their vice president strode forward and shared some company history that only the old-timers were aware of. Back in the early 1980s, this organization had been on the brink of bankruptcy, but they survived and rebounded. As he described this recovery, I could see faces brightening and shoulders straightening throughout the room. They were discovering a newfound strength in themselves. "Yes," the vice president continued, "we're having a tough time, but if we could make it then, we can make it now." He went on to paint a vivid picture of where the company was going.

My valued friend and mentor, Dave Lucchetti, is president and CEO of Pacific Coast Building Products, a very successful construction supply company based in California. As chief executive, he has had to manage the inevitable peaks and valleys of the general economy as well as the ups and downs of the building industry.

How does he do this? Because he has always used adversity as a learning opportunity, he's now able to remain buoyant during turbulent times. Dave has developed the survivor's edge. He told me, "I've learned that when there is a recession, I don't have to participate." His philosophy is, "If you want to remain resilient in life and work, the past is a good place to visit, but you don't want to live there." Dave has taught me that the key is to use past experience to guide future actions and to strengthen our resilience.

Some events can't be foreseen or prevented, and their occurrence may offer little guidance for future actions. To paraphrase a popular bumper sticker, "Stuff happens." When negative events happen unexpectedly in your life, whether in a business setting like Dave's or in an intensely personal situation like Lisa's, your first questions should be:

- Could I have predicted this?
- Could I have prevented this?
- Should this affect my future actions?

If you can honestly answer "probably not" to all three questions, then you're a candidate for an *Adversity Insurance Dividend:* discovering that you can endure.

Building Block #4—Your Past Victories

My friend Del "Doc" Anderson was in his seventies when his car had a head-on collision with a truck. After he'd been in a deep coma for three weeks, the doctors gently told his family that he probably would not recover.

His family, however, never gave up. At the nurses' suggestion, they sat talking to Doc day after day, reminiscing about people and places he had known.

One Saturday afternoon, twenty-four days after the accident, Doc's son Keith was in Doc's room watching a Cal-Berkeley football game on the little TV set over the bed. Since Doc had played football for Cal, it was a family tradition to watch every game.

Toward the end of the first quarter, Doc opened his eyes. He couldn't talk because he'd had a tracheotomy, but he mouthed the words "Who's playing?"

The cheers that erupted in that hospital room were as loud as those in the stadium. Later, when he could talk again, Doc told me, "I always said that when the coach said, 'Go in to play,' I'd be ready." Doc's now in his eighties—and he still never misses a Cal-Berkeley game.

No matter who you are, no matter what you've done, you've been more courageous than you know. Sometimes it takes courage just to get out of bed and face a difficult situation. Give yourself credit for that. Sometimes courage is doing the only thing possible, given the options. People who have been incredibly courageous often express astonishment that anyone would wonder how they did it. "What else could I do?" they ask.

Courage doesn't come from committees. It's an individual commitment, although it's often contagious. Real courage isn't looking for dragons to slay or rapids to run. Real courage is when you keep going despite fear, pain, or failure. I've found that when I confront what I fear, I end up more powerful.

Your greatest accomplishments are completely different from everyone else's. You can't compare yours to mine and neither of us can productively compare our achievements to those of anyone else. For example, most children are able to tie their shoes when they are about five years old. I was sixteen before I learned to tie my own shoelaces, using much creativity and persistence. We can judge our own progress only by comparing where we were in the past and where are now.

Olympic swimmer Janet Evans went from winning a gold medal in the 400-meters freestyle in 1988 to winning a silver medal in the same event in 1992. She told me that she was stunned when some sports commentators suggested that she had "lost," that being second best in the world was hardly good enough. Yet, the 1992 gold-medal winner had failed to surpass Janet's 1988 gold-medal time! Janet told me that when she views her past, she's as proud of that 1992 silver medal as of her 1988 gold because it took tremendous intensity and effort to requalify for the team. "When you're at the top, it is harder to motivate yourself to stay there," Janet says.

How does this relate to the rest of us? Success is not *being* the best but *doing* our best. Few of us are going to be gold medalists, but we still have to celebrate our unique achievements with "mental medals." Sometimes we use photos, certificates, and other external reminders of past achievements, but mental medals can be more enduring and easier to carry about with us. By noticing what we've done right, we create an inventory of past attainments to sustain and encourage us when things go wrong.

When people are really down, they have a hard time remembering what they have accomplished. A business owner who goes bankrupt may see every past achievement as worthless because it didn't prevent the current setback. The person whose marriage breaks up after twenty years may dismiss those two decades as "wasted," forgetting the rich, productive years that preceded the rift. Someone who loses everything in an earthquake, fire, or flood may see his or her life as purposeless because everything vanished so easily. They temporarily lose sight of their real legacy: the self-esteem, strengths, skills, knowledge, laughter, passion, tears, and joy they have experienced along the way.

That's why the best time to collect mental medals is when you're feeling positive and upbeat. Then they're there when you need to draw strength from them.

BOUNCE HIGHER TIP

*Memorialize your past accomplishments
with mental medals now
for use when your resilience is low.*

Building Block #5—Images from Your Childhood

One of my most precious childhood memories is captured in a picture that hangs in my office. I've often drawn strength from this image, a true mental medal.

One crisp fall morning, when I'd been in elementary school for only a few weeks, the teacher instructed us to take a piece of paper from our desks. The teacher passed around a tray of thick, red paint so we could make handprints on the paper. I remember thrusting my hands down in the shallow baking pan and feeling the cold paint ooze over my fingers. Then I carefully pressed them on the paper. Later, when the paint was dry, we all put our names on our handprints. I proudly wrote my name at the bottom of the page: Roger Crawford.

When I got home, I carefully removed the piece of paper from my backpack and unfolded it. The love and pride in my parents' eyes was obvious. My father, who has a delightful sense of humor, said, "Roger, I'm glad you printed your name at the bottom, or else we wouldn't have known they were yours." Then he said, "Let's take a picture." My mother knelt on one knee and placed her arm around my waist. She was wearing her familiar red-and-white apron with eyelet trim. Then I put my left arm on her shoulder and tilted my head so it rested against her cheek. "One, two, three," my father exclaimed, and the flashbulb popped. Years later, this photo still inspires me as I see my mother holding up my handprints with a smile that says "I'm glad you're my son."

My friend Barry Spanjaard used childhood memories to survive the unspeakable horrors of Auschwitz during World War II. When the torture, starvation, and cold became too much to bear, he would visualize special times with his parents and playing with his friends in his backyard. These compelling images from his past gave him the strength to cope with the present.

He told me that when the guards would bring the prisoners soup that looked and tasted like dirty water, he'd see his mother bringing him a steaming bowl of matzoh-ball soup. Then he'd taste the rich chicken broth and feel the tender matzoh balls melting on his tongue. If he was given a crust of moldy bread, he'd smell the perfume of his mother's fresh-baked rolls and sense the warmth on his fingers as he tore them apart and slathered on the melting yellow butter. This sustained him. "I noticed," he told me, "that when others around me began to lose hope, they stopped trying to visualize. Without something—*anything*—positive from the past to hold on to, that's when they started to fall apart."

Starting Over

"Who are you?" Many people answer that question by saying, "I'm a teacher" or "I'm a truck driver." But businesses change, downsize, and close. Technology changes. People change. How would you react if you arrived at your job tomorrow and there was no job? Would you still know who you are? Would you be able to draw on your past to reinvent yourself if you had to find a new profession?

From Bricks to Bread

In the 1980s, Lou Statzer was a very successful real-estate developer in the Washington, D.C., area. Then, in 1990, the real-estate market declined sharply and Lou faced bankruptcy. "I almost lost everything," he says. "There I was with no college education, unemployed, and more or less unhirable."

Lou had to take stock of his resources, including his past achievements. Fortunately, his past demonstrated that he was a skilled entrepreneur, able to recognize potential markets and to build from the bottom. At the age of twenty, he had started a one-man office on a shoestring, selling calculators, typewriters, and the new small computers. In seven years, he built his backroom service into a lucrative chain of six stores with one hundred employees. Then, in his late twenties, Lou decided to retire to the Caribbean! He sold his business, bought a sailboat, and moved to St. Thomas. After three months, he was bored, so he started a local Jeep-rental business. Soon he had a chain of rental agencies throughout the Caribbean. Seven years later, he was bored again, so he returned to the U.S. and made good in the red-hot real-estate market.

Then, red-hot turned ice-cold and Lou lost everything. For the first time in his life, he found himself involuntarily unemployed and forced to start over from scratch. His personal resilience in this crisis demonstrates that there are two kinds of people: those who are poor and those who are simply without money. He began to look around for a new area to conquer. Like all great entrepreneurs, he followed the dictum, Find a need and fill it. Lou loves good bread, but he'd never been able to find any in Washington, D.C. He reasoned that Washingtonians might patronize a bakery that sold hot, fragrant loaves of top-quality bread.

His first step, based on past experience, was to go to the source. He tracked down the manufacturer of the world's best stone-hearth steam-injected bread ovens. They were located, naturally, in France, a country where superb bread is a national passion. Lou promised to buy his equipment exclusively from them if they would give him the name of the world's best baker. They gave him two names. One gentleman was in Japan, the other in Saratoga Springs, New York.

Lou jumped in his car and drove from Washington, D.C., to Saratoga Springs. There he found Michael London, a baking genius who has made bread his life. (London's dedication included spending several years in Italy learning about Italian bread and several years in California perfecting his sourdough.) London had never shared his secrets before, but Lou was highly persuasive.

Back in Washington, Lou opened a small bakery in the Cleveland Park neighborhood. Customers immediately responded to the excellence of his product and he soon went from two employees to a hundred. "They're the highest paid in the industry," says Lou, "plus great benefits, so there is a lot of employee loyalty. Every worker starts as a counterperson, driver, or dishwasher, and then works up within the company, so they really feel involved with the company."

Although Lou loves working at the front counter, he's now tied up with maintaining quality control for his round-the-clock business, which bakes, packs, and delivers bread twenty-four hours a day. Uptown Bakers currently offers seventeen kinds of bread, from casareccio to raisin-pecan. Unless people stop eating bread, he is unlikely to have to change careers again. Will he get bored and want new horizons? "There are so many facets to really great bread and so much potential for diversification," he says, "that I can't imagine wanting to do something else. This is probably 'it.' "

The unresilient look back at their past and collect evidence of rejection and failure, discarding examples of acceptance and proficiency. People who maintain their resilience have a memory bank in which they deposit all the times when they were challenged but successfully managed the difficulty. They invest their life experiences in this account. Then, whenever adversity strikes, they can live on their investments.

PROFILE

Gail Ptacek

One day Gail Hummel Ptacek was in charge of a staff of twenty. The next day, she and many of her fellow employees were scanning the Help Wanted ads. It's become a common story, but statistics can't take the sting out of being forced to reinvent yourself. Gail had started out as a nurse in Illinois, using her master's degree in public and health-care administration to become assistant head nurse of an ambulatory surgery unit. When she moved to California and couldn't find a comparable position, her degree helped her switch to the business end of health care.

During eleven years in the managed-health-care industry, Gail worked her way up to be the Northern California director of operations for a major insurance company. Then came a merger and mass layoffs. Two months after her fortieth birthday, Gail was unemployed and taking stock of her past—her experiences, skills, talents, interests, and goals. "I started by looking for a job doing what I'd been doing, but everyone in our industry was merging. More and more skilled, experienced people were out of work."

As part of her outplacement package, Gail made a background survey of her interests and abilities. Many, she discovered, fell in areas outside the health-care industry. "So," she recalls, "since health care no longer had a place for me, I decided to do something else that I enjoyed."

Gail had been cooking "since I was big enough to reach a stove. It was something I've always loved," she says. She had written some sample cooking columns, but had never tried to sell them. Syndicating a column profitably is an iffy business, but Gail decided she'd never have a better time to try. She went to work, writing and self-syndicating the column. In the first six months, "Gail's Galley" sold to twelve newspapers. "I still had to do occasional health-care consulting to pay the rent," she says, "but now the column is really taking off." "Gail's Galley" is expanding into radio and into annual recipe collections marketed through the column.

Gail Ptacek consciously used the building blocks of her past to reinvent herself and her future. By assessing your past successes, mistakes, adversities, victories, and even images from your childhood, you can find extra resilience in unexpected situations. You'll be able to maintain positive, proactive attitudes because you'll have already built a solid foundation of resilience.

R E S I L I E N C E   B U I L D E R

Banking on Your Past

America is a nation of immigrants and children of immigrants, many of whom came here to get away from a past that was holding them down. It's now become a national trait to ignore the inequities and inadequacies of the past, focusing on what's right right now and what's ahead.

This admirable ideal ignores a rich heritage that we can all profitably draw on. (Whether we like it or not, as Shakespeare noted, "What's past is prologue.") Our resilience starts by recognizing and celebrating both the positive *and* the negative from our pasts. Whenever you face difficult situations, it helps to look back on how you overcame similar challenges in the past. What skills did you use then?

1. Identify Your Past Successes and Accomplishments

Remember that they can come in very small packages. You can draw an abundance of energy from small daily successes as well as major, life-enhancing accomplishments. Warm up for your self-inventory by listing thirty (yes, thirty!) things you've set out to do and eventually done. Put an X next to five successes that required internal boldness. Do you notice any similarities or consistent themes?

2. Identify Your Past Mistakes

Choose three things you did or failed to do in the past that you now feel were "mistakes." Describe what you learned from the experiences. How has this understanding changed how you will act in the future?

3. Identify Your Past Victories over Adversities

List ten events that really hurt or seemed overwhelming at the time: big or small failures, losses, accidents, illnesses, even stupid or embarrassing mistakes. These are your adversities. Then go back and jot down the processes and resources you used to *recover.* For example:

- I figured out a solution.
- I reevaluated the situation.
- I focused on the event.
- I ignored the event and focused on other things.
- I sought the help or advice of others.
- The passage of time helped heal the wound.

These are your victories. Evaluate the success of these strategies. If a similar situation occurred in the future, would you try a different strategy?

4. Identify Your Past Joys

Which of your accomplishments or achievements have given you the most satisfaction or feeling of importance? (You can repeat items from your #1 list.) Remember that friendship and loving family relationships are true accomplishments, and often our greatest joys.

5. Identify Your "Future Past"

We tend to become precisely what we imagine ourselves to be. What in your past predicts your future? How? What control do you have over this self-image?

Wisdom on Wheels

"Boy, I love traffic!" cried my good friend, Dave Dohrman, and he threw back his head and laughed. Our car was stuck in bumper-to-bumper rush-hour traffic, so I began to worry about his sanity.

We were on our way to the convention center near Detroit where I was scheduled to speak at a Farmers Insurance regional meeting. Dave, who has one of their top agencies, was acting as my host. He had picked me up at my hotel in plenty of time, but now we were gridlocked. I admit to a low tolerance for heavy traffic, so, as Dave continued to chuckle and smile, I wondered if he was feeling well. How could *anyone* enjoy a traffic jam?

"Yes," he said cheerfully, "I especially like to get into a backup on my way to work in the morning. It stimulates and motivates me for the whole day." By now, Dave had convinced me he was absolutely bonkers. Then he explained.

"You see, Roger, traffic jams used to really get me down. Then I realized I had a choice about my attitude. Now when I'm in a traffic jam like this and I look at all those people in all those cars, I think of the incredible potential I have. They're all customers who haven't bought car insurance from me yet!"

PART TWO

"How Long Have You Been There?"

YOUR SELF-IMAGE

Rio! No film or snapshot image can prepare you for the view of Sugarloaf Mountain from the plane window. I had arrived a day early for an international sales conference so I'd have time to get over jet lag and see something of this fabled and fabulous city. The names alone—Ipanema, Copacabaña, the *cariocas*—are as musical as the songs they've inspired. Exhausted after the long flight, I was soon lulled to sleep in my hotel room by the distinctive rhythms of car horns competing with bicycle bells.

Early the next morning I was off with an English-speaking guide, marveling at the unreal blue of the ocean, the ultramodern buildings, the contrast of sleek, diesel-powered Mercedes limos sweeping past flocks of cyclists and the occasional donkey cart. I

was overwhelmed by the incredible natural crescent of Copacabaña Beach, the sudden splashes of brilliantly colored flowers,
and the rich variety of faces, a mingling of indigenous peoples with
descendants of Portuguese, African, Lebanese, Syrian, and Japanese immigrants.

Toward the end of my tour, I asked my guide if there was somewhere we could get a panoramic view of the city. He nodded and
soon our car turned off one of the spacious avenues and began
winding upward. We passed handsome middle-class homes with
well-kept gardens. Then the road became bumpier. The wheel-
alignment business in Rio must be very profitable, I thought.

As we climbed, the potholes grew more and more frequent, and
the comfortable homes gave way to the most desperately impover-
ished area I've ever seen. In most cities built on hills, the poor
cluster at the bottom, while the rich live uphill with the cleaner air
and the grander views. In Rio, however, it is the poorest inhabi-
tants who cling to the sides of what many call the most beautiful
hills in the world.

We drove through a tangle of tightly packed shelters so
crammed together that each seemed to be holding up its neighbor. These huts were ingeniously crafted from a hodgepodge of
flattened oil drums, plastic sheeting, broken furniture, cardboard,
metal bedsprings, and hundreds of other objects that can be
found in any American city dump. Anything remotely like clean
drinking water or sanitation seemed to be nonexistent. Competing for space in this squalid jumble were thousands of ill-clad, ill-
fed people.

Our car reached the top of a hill overlooking the bay. As I
stepped out, a wonderfully cool breeze hit my face. I turned to look
at the view and was overwhelmed. For the first time I really understood what breathtaking meant. Far below was the harbor, unbe-
lievably blue and dotted with tiny white sails. Beyond that, the
sweeping curve of Copacabaña Beach and Ipanema Beach. Three
miles to the right was the summit of Corcovado (the "Hunch-
back"), topped by the giant statue of Jesus with arms outstretched.

I grabbed my camera and started to frame a photo of this incredible scene. As I turned slowly, looking for the best shot, my viewfinder picked up a woman and two children trudging up the hill. The woman and little girl wore tattered T-shirts and skirts, the boy only threadbare shorts, much too big for him and cinched in at the waist with a cord. All were barefoot. Despite their obvious poverty, they were stunningly handsome, with the gorgeous bronze skin and jet-black hair of their Indian ancestors. I lowered my camera for a moment to smile at them, then started to focus on Corcovado in the distance.

The mother thought I was going to take their picture. Quickly she ran a hand over her windblown hair and then grabbed the hem of her frayed shirt. With that universal maternal gesture, she spit on it and began scrubbing the dusty faces of her children. They squirmed the way all kids do, but there is no escaping a mother's headlock. Then she said something to them, and all three smiled proudly, waiting for me to take their picture. This wasn't just a smile. This was an ear-to-ear grin that would have made the most cynical sourpuss smile back. As I snapped the picture, they were standing tall and proud in the lower left-hand corner.

When I got back in the car, I waved to them and all three waved back. As my guide and I jounced down the hill, I couldn't stop thinking about them. Here were people who seemed to have every reason in the world not to smile. They clearly had a hard life and lacked the simplest necessities. Yet their smiles demonstrated an incredible joy.

Suddenly I realized that these people had an essential component of resilience: a sense of self-worth. It was exemplified by the mother's quick swipes at her children's smudged faces and her murmured words to stand up straight and smile. She was telling her children with actions louder than words:

No matter what your circumstances, you have value.

What a critically important message: "You're valuable." "You're beautiful." "You have intrinsic worth." Even in such poverty, this mother gave her children pride and a sense of importance.

I took several rolls of film during my stay in South America, but the most cherished picture I have is of that family. They were the most beautiful sight I saw in Brazil.

"How Long Have You Been There?"

How you answer the border guard's second question, "How long have you been there?" is central to your self-image. It's not necessary to have a prestigious family tree to have a profound sense of personal value. And no matter how great (or small) your public recognition and reputation, true self-worth comes from your personal inner wealth, your "reputation with yourself."

Your self-image represents who and what you believe yourself to be, your core beliefs about your strengths and weaknesses, possibilities and limitations. Facing life's bumps and bruises without the armor of a positive self-image is a tremendous handicap. When life is unstable, we must find the stability within ourselves. If attitudes are the foundation of resilience, your self-image represents the structural walls.

Here's the good news. If you feel you're trapped in a cycle of poor self-image and low resilience, you can break out! You are never too young or too old to change your self-image. The next three chapters will give you strategies to increase your inner wealth and inner bounce. Remember that you are unique. Too many of us overrate other people's abilities and underrate our own. Billions of people have walked this earth, but there's never been, nor will there ever be, anyone exactly like you. Don't undervalue yourself!

A Renewable Resource

Some people think that once you acquire a positive self-image, it's yours forever. That would be wonderful, but unfortunately our self-image is constantly buffeted and eroded by daily events. It can fluctuate from day to day, influencing your ability to stay adaptable, happy, and positive. The stronger and more resilient your self-image is, the better equipped you are to maintain your buoyancy during turbulent times.

Fortunately, you can keep your self-image in pretty good shape by an artful combination of flattery and hardheaded self-analysis. When you're doing a realistic evaluation of your shortcomings and setbacks, be sure to balance it with copious compliments on your talents and successes. Dr. Robert Schuller says, "Don't waste time putting yourself down. There'll be plenty of other people happy to do it for you."

A teacher once told me a delightful story. Her students were making Halloween masks for a class play. One little girl, who was in a wheelchair, confided to her teacher that she was concerned her parents might not recognize her. This girl didn't see herself as a child-in-a-wheelchair, but simply as a child who had made a magical mask.

You increase your sense of self-worth whenever you do new things to stretch you and develop new skills and capabilities. The question "How long have I been there?" provides a continual evaluation of your progress.

Truly resilient people are constantly updating the scripts of their lives to reemphasize the worth of their core values. Even if they've experienced a severe setback or loss, they can write this into the script of their lives. Just as a forest is replanted after logging, resilient people figure out ways to replace what has been taken from them by time or circumstances.

Your Second Set of Keys

The next three chapters are about how your *self-image* affects your resilience.

4. Stay Hungry. Seek knowledge, adventure, and friendship.

5. Use All Your Resources. Your wealth is far greater than you imagine.

6. Seize Responsibility. Your most dependable ally is *you*.

The best time to put up storm windows or to strengthen your self-image is before the storm hits. Once you understand the full scope of your personal resources, you are fortified against whatever life throws at you.

The resilient people you'll read about in the next three chapters are very different from one another, but they all have one thing in common. They were all hungry for personal growth, they were all resourceful, and they all made themselves ultimately responsible for their own resilience.

4

Stay Hungry

BUILD YOUR INTERNAL WEALTH

I was looking back at seventy-five pairs of eyes belonging to some of the youngest criminals in the country. A corporate client of mine had asked me to speak at a juvenile detention center where he often volunteered his time to help troubled youngsters. These weren't just runaways and mixed-up kids. All these teenagers had broken the law.

As I started to talk to them, I looked into their eyes and saw enormous sadness. Most of them had lived such difficult lives, lives so different from mine. I realized just how different when one young man stood up during the question-and-answer session. "Roger," he asked, "when you're arrested, how do they handcuff you?"

That same day, another inmate at the detention center said something that profoundly changed how I think about life. She was only about sixteen, but she plainly had packed a lot of life experience into her years. I was surprised to learn that she came from a rather wealthy family.

This teenager told me about her parents, successful professionals who worked long hours. Often they wouldn't get home until late at night, and she spent many evenings alone. She told me how much she had missed them, and how she would get into trouble so they would pay attention to her. Each time, they told her that they were working hard to give her all the things they never had when they were growing up. As we talked, this girl kept staring at her hands in her lap. Then suddenly she looked up at me. *"Roger, all I ever wanted from my parents is what they had."*

I asked her to explain. She told me that her parents always insisted they were "doing it all for her," but all she ever wanted was their love, attention, and encouragement. She had lots of "things," but not the things she needed. In a simple and profound way, she made me see the role of hunger in all our lives and the difference between being hungry for money and being hungry for inner wealth.

Stay Hungry for True Wealth

Do you know the difference between money and wealth? Money can be taken from you at any time, but your wealth is yours forever. Resilient people are invariably wealthy. They "own" what is valuable to them and can never lose it.

A house burns down. A company ceases operations. A loved one dies. Any of these is a terrible loss, but for resilient people the real wealth remains. Nothing and no one can rob them of the experiences, skills, and rewards of creating a home, a business, or a loving relationship. The unresilient dwell on what is gone, what can never be again. When they do consider the future, it is usually to plan how they can avoid pain: "I'll never work that hard again for anyone," or "I won't risk loving someone else that much."

Resilient people hurt just as much. However, they are eventually able to draw strength from their proven abilities to build, work, and love. Usually these skills are still intact. If not, resilient people can still recall them with pride, using them as a starting point for building new resources of mind and spirit.

So many of us go through life thinking that the next raise, the next promotion, or the next acquisition will make our lives complete. Just a little more of what we've got now and we'll be perfectly happy. We confuse having the best with being the best.

Unresilient people usually measure themselves by comparing what they have to what they think others have, both materially and personally. For them, the grass is always greener somewhere else. Ironically, whenever we decide that happiness and contentment depend on having what others seem to have, or in having *more* than others seem to have, failure is guaranteed. Contentment is impossible because there will always be someone who seems richer, thinner, or more successful. True self-esteem can never be created externally by what you wear, do, drive, live in, or own.

If you were a fan of the TV series *Dallas*, you may recall the episode where the enormously rich and powerful J.R. has been committed to a mental institution by his enemies. When he finally gets out, he is a changed man. He tells a sympathetic listener that he had always thought his money and power would protect him from everything, "but now I've learned that's not true." The listener nods understandingly. "Yes," continues J.R. with a malevolent grin, "I've learned that I'm just going to have to be even richer and more powerful so this will never happen to me again!" Undoubtedly, some people will always confuse money and wealth. They are fixated on acquisition—what they call security. However, as the Reverend Billy Graham often says, "I've presided at many funerals, and I have never seen a U-HAUL attached to a hearse."

Olympic speed-skating medal-winner Dan Jansen illustrates the real difference between money and wealth. Dan comes from a large family. When he was a child, one of his friends got a new pair of expensive skates. Dan asked his parents for similar skates, but they couldn't afford them. "Are we poor?" Dan asked his father. His father answered, "As long as we've got nine children, we're rich."

James Dobson, who does the syndicated radio show *Focus on the Family*, summed it up best for me: "I have concluded that the accumulation of riches, even if I could achieve them, is an insufficient reason for living. . . . I will consider my earthly existence to have been wasted unless I can recall a loving family, a consistent investment in the lives of people, and an earnest attempt to serve the God who made us. *Nothing else makes much sense.*"

BOUNCE HIGHER TIP

Develop your internal wealth.
It's the safe that can't be cracked.

True wealth consists of what no one can steal from you: knowledge, for one, and real-life adventures and experiences that increase your internal boldness; opportunities noticed and seized; and the most precious and life-sustaining wealth of all, friendship, love, and intimacy.

Stay Hungry for Knowledge

How's your appetite for learning? Right this minute, you have access to more knowledge than any monarch or millionaire in the history of the world. No matter who you are, in our society there are no laws or customs that can prevent you from learning everything you want to know. You can be poorer than a church mouse and live in the most remote part of the world, but can still access the accumulated knowledge of humanity if you want to. Even being blind or deaf or both can't block an eager mind from experiencing the enormous wealth of science, history, art, and language.

Pay as much attention to what you feed your mind as you do to what you feed your body. It is possible to starve a mind or weaken it with a steady diet of junk food. Information is simply the raw material of knowledge, rather like the food products on the shelves of a giant supermarket. Knowledge is what you choose to put in your shopping cart, take home, cook, serve, and digest. Knowledge represents your own highly individual choices for selecting, evaluating, and arranging the ingredients. Fortunately, the quality and variety of these ingredients have never been greater.

"The Immigrant Mentality"

One of the most inspiring people I've ever met is Nido Qubein. Nido came to the U.S. from Lebanon at the age of eighteen, unable to speak English. Four years later he graduated from High Point University in North Carolina, and went on to earn a doctorate and become a very successful businessman. One quality I most admire in Nido is his eagerness for knowledge. He says, "I've always possessed the immigrant mentality. I'm going to take everything that America has to offer—the freedom to learn, the freedom to achieve."

Nido told me that he invests his time three ways: one-third for learning, one-third for earning, and one-third for serving. Even much of his serving relates to learning because he is a board member of fifteen educational and charitable organizations, and founder of the Nido Qubein Scholarship Fund, which has awarded more than three hundred educational grants to deserving college students from the High Point area.

When Nido took me home to meet his family, I was impressed that his four children, ages five to sixteen, all rushed to hug and kiss him. (That's true wealth!) He describes himself as someone "who truly cherishes the joy of living."

Later, I visited his children's school. The headmaster pointed to the school library. "Dr. Qubein donated that building and all those books because he said the key to these children's futures is in these books." Nido is making sure that thousands of children can make the same investments that rewarded him so richly.

Resilient people share this "immigrant mentality," no matter where they are born or live.

As you sharpen your appetite for knowledge, here are five ways to appease your hunger:

1. Listen!

A young woman in the front row of an IBM sales meeting caught my eye. She was professionally dressed in a tailored red suit and white blouse, with neatly coiffed hair and glasses, but it wasn't her appearance that I noticed as much as what she was doing. She was listening! And she was taking copious notes as the regional sales manager made his presentation. She continued to take notes when I spoke. I pegged her as a new employee, eager to learn the ropes.

At the end of the meeting, awards were handed out to the top salespeople, starting with number five and working up to number one. Number one in the district was Deborah Jane Turner. She stood up to acknowledge the applause. As you've probably guessed, she was my "beginner," the lady in the red suit.

Deborah Jane Turner showed me why she was the best. We may sometimes compete against others and win, but the real pleasure comes in raising ourselves above our current level of performance.

What would you pay to have access to the output of five hundred million minds on several thousand subjects covering a time period of eons and a geographical area larger than our planet? Guess what? It's free! All you have to do is listen.

While some people hunt hungrily for gold or oil, resilient people are hungry to explore the minds and opinions of others, from janitors to CEO's, and they know their daughter's day-care worker might say the most profound thing they will hear today.

2. Ask Questions!

I learned about the importance of questions from one of the best. He's Arthur Mirante, president and CEO of one of the largest commercial real-estate firms in the United States, Cushman & Wakefield. Arthur was reviewing strategies for the coming year at a brokers' meeting in New York. Suddenly, one of the sales managers stood up and said, "Excuse me, Arthur. I'm embarrassed to say that I am not completely clear on this point." Arthur was already my friend and mentor, but he really earned my respect and admiration with his reply. "Don't be embarrassed," he said. "If you're going to be a leader, you must never be afraid to say you don't understand something."

For peak performers, school is never out. They are lifelong scholars. Some people think they can stop learning when they walk out the school door, but resilient folks never lose their childlike curiosity about the world.

How many times have you been in a situation where someone (maybe you) said, "I'm not really clear about that. Could you go over it again?" Chances are there were a lot of grateful sighs from others who'd also been struggling to understand, but who were reluctant to say anything. They were more afraid of seeming unintelligent or inattentive than of the consequences of not understanding. Their hunger for the good opinion of others surpassed their hunger to know.

But what if the point is reexplained and you still don't understand? Remember that different people process information in different ways. A hungry person may say, "I'm still not entirely clear. Perhaps you could illustrate that." (Or "demonstrate" or "list the steps" or "define your terms" or "give some background" or even "Can you clarify what will be different for *us* when this policy goes into effect?")

Resilient people are so hungry to learn that they are willing to trade a few minutes of temporary discomfort for permanent knowledge. They're so eager to learn from others that they readily admit they don't know everything. They ask lots of questions, even supposedly dumb ones. Fragile people don't want to appear foolish or incompetent, but their silence can convey just that.

One of the paradoxes of a resilient life is that the more we learn, the more we recognize that we still need to learn. When you want and need relevant information and you actively seek it out, asking questions and listening to the answers, that information is locked into your memory more powerfully than by any other method. It becomes yours for life.

Questioners win two ways. Not only do they learn something, but they are giving an incredible gift. They let others feel important and smart. When you ask people for information or advice, you are telling them they're valuable and that they have significant knowledge and opinions. Most of us like to be around people who make us feel good about ourselves. Which kind of person would you rather be with? Someone who appears distant and disinterested when you talk? Or someone who responds with enthusiastic questions that allow you to show off your expertise?

After all your information collecting, the most important question of all is, "Where does this fit in the larger scheme of things?" Random bits of information may be fairly useless unless you see them as important parts of a bigger pattern. Go for the "why" as well as the "what." It's amazing how much information you can process and store when you use it to fill in the big picture.

3. Read!

A few hundred years ago, the majority of the world's population was illiterate. It was nearly impossible to share ideas quickly or across geographical distances. Nowadays, if you can read, you possess a skill that gives you access to the wisdom of thousands of years and the experiences of billions of other human beings. A single issue of a major metropolitan newspaper contains more information than someone in the sixteenth century encountered in a lifetime.

BOUNCE HIGHER TIP

If you can read and don't,
you might as well be illiterate.

4. Watch!

In our electronic age, exposure to what the rest of the world has to offer isn't limited to the printed page. Films, television, video-tapes, and the Internet offer almost instant access to more infor-mation and viewpoints than all the libraries of the world contained just a few decades ago. Many people learn more easily if they can see an example, and many processes are more easily shown than explained.

5. Stay Open to New Ideas!

Resilient people are fascinated by the infinite range of discoveries and by differing human responses to the same facts and events. They don't feel threatened when they read or talk about new ideas, so they constantly enrich themselves with new discoveries and insights.

"My mind is made up, don't confuse me with facts," could be the motto of the unresilient. Resilient people have their internal landmarks and "givens," but they can tolerate far more ambiguity and blurring of edges than nonresilient people can. They're confi-dent about the general rightness of their belief systems, and they stay open to better ways of thinking about and looking at things.

One of the hungriest people for continuous improvement I know is Harvey Mackay. He was already the head of a major company (the Mackay Envelope Corporation), author of a world-famous best-seller *(Swim with the Sharks without Being Eaten Alive)*, and—most impressive from my point of view—a tennis champion ranked in the senior division in Minnesota. Yet, at the age of fifty, Mackay felt he needed a challenge. He decided to become a marathon runner.

His approach was the same one he'd used to achieve success in business and publishing. He learned everything he could. Run-ning twenty-six miles without stopping isn't something you under-take lightly. First he read extensively about running and training techniques. Then he sought the best coaching available. He viewed videos on different aspects of running and watched newscasts of local and national races to learn which runners were competing in marathons, where, when, and how. He was hungry to know everything about the subject as he prepared himself mentally, physically, and spiritually. When he was ready, he ran the marathon, all twenty-six miles, and, as he expected, he finished.

"Become hungry and assertive in seeking advice from people that you admire," Harvey says. "When I am embarking on a new adventure, I seek out the best available mentors that I have encountered throughout my life. What I have found fascinating is the more successful people are, the more likely they are to give you advice that you are actively seeking."

Some of us are too shy to approach others because "they'd be offended" or "they're too busy," but Harvey says that's rarely true. Even if you've been turned down once or twice, don't let that stop you. Successful people usually understand the perseverance it takes to be successful and they're willing to lend a hand or offer advice. Be tenacious. Find people who have had similar challenges and had the resilience to meet them. Seek the best advice you can get. You deserve it!

Stay Hungry for Adventure

People with high self-regard are excited about venturing into the unknown. They embrace risks rather than running from them. They are stimulated by the challenge and excitement of worthwhile, demanding goals. When these goals are reached, their self-image is further enhanced. That's why they're often willing to gamble security and comfort for adventure, knowledge, and opportunities.

Of course, being resilient doesn't mean putting yourself in dangerous situations for a thrill. But stretching your comfort zone in productive ways is a constant source of energy, growth, and self-esteem.

Unresilient people are usually "risk-averse." They play not to lose and end up not winning. Resilient people play to win. They are hungry for opportunities, win, lose, or draw. But if a salesperson's low resilience inhibits the "cold calls" necessary for success, he won't put himself in the situations where sales are made. If a manager is reluctant to make presentations, she has little chance of becoming a skilled communicator and motivator. A hunger for challenges, even if you risk rejection or failure, is resilience in action.

A Tennis Lesson

As a teaching tennis professional, I've had the opportunity to study risk taking on a stroke-by-stroke basis. Unresilient people feel that if they don't try, they can't lose. But sit on the sidelines and you are assured of losing. I used to tell players, "You miss 100 percent of the shots you don't take." If you want to be in the match at all, you have to risk losing. When I think about the connection between resilience and risk, I remember two very different young men.

"John" was sixteen when I first began to coach him. He had a fine athletic build, wore only top-brand tennis wear, and used the latest Wilson Profile racket. When he played a match, people would comment on his fluid strokes and his agility on the court. Expectations for him were extremely high. At the very least, he would earn a tennis scholarship at a prestigious university.

"Bill" was the complete opposite. When he arrived for practice, he looked as if he had slept in his clothes, and his equipment was outdated. His strokes were unorthodox and his court speed was limited, but I admired him for his tenacity and commitment to learning everything he could about his game. He spent hours reviewing videotapes of all the great players and took copious notes. Then he'd carry some of those notes in his sock so he could review them during the match.

John never spent time on extra preparation. He preferred hitting balls with others rather than playing matches. This way he could play it safe and preserve his reputation as an abundantly gifted player. Bill, on the other hand, enjoyed competition and played matches every chance he got. He was constantly placing his self-image "at risk," challenging himself to improve. He lost a lot of games, but he learned something every time. And rather than damaging his self-image and resilience, such losses raised them and made him stronger.

Now, I'm not saying that everyone has to be a supercompetitor. Some people play just for the joy of it, and that's a form of personal success. The point is that John wasn't one of these people. Even though he tried to cut his losses by not competing, he still experienced a high level of stress. His parents were the kind who lived vicariously through their children, and he was constantly worried about failing to meet their expectations. He was viewed by others and by himself as someone who had squandered a great ability and tossed away opportunities for a tennis scholarship and a successful tennis career. By playing not to lose, he lost on every level.

Right now you're expecting me to tell you that Bill went on to fame and glory as a tennis champion while John came to a sad end. I can't tell you that because I don't know what happened to John, but I do know what happened to Bill. He now owns a successful chain of pasta restaurants. That may seem pretty far from the tennis court, but Bill doesn't think so. He feels his ability to manage the peaks and valleys of being an entrepreneur is directly related to the resilience he learned as a young tennis player.

BOUNCE HIGHER TIP

Play to win, not to avoid losing.

Stay Hungry for Friendship

Here's a paradox: Even though you create your own self-image, resilience is rarely a solo effort. We all need support, encouragement, and inspiration from those around us. The quality of these relationships determines the quality of our lives. We all need genuine friends, the kind that walk in when others walk out. A strong life is stronger with such friends.

Nothing can erode self-worth and resilience faster than toxic, destructive relationships. Seek out friends who are constantly helping you become what you know you are capable of, who want the BEST for you. They:

B - believe in you
E - encourage you
S - support you
T - trust you

You can't choose your relatives and you can't always choose the people you live and work with, but you can always choose which of your acquaintances to make your friends.

As a student of resilience, I've noticed that people with the ability to bounce back and to bounce higher have a social network they call on in both good and bad times. We all enjoy being around resilient people. Their optimism brightens the day of strangers and is a source of sustenance to their friends and loved ones. They are the spark plugs for other people's enthusiasm and resilience, as well as their own.

When you're feeling unresilient, the usual advice is to find a friend who is a sympathetic and attentive listener. I'll add to that. Be sure to choose someone who is optimistic and uplifting. A fellow moan-and-groaner isn't going to help you. Nor is a friend who offers false assurances. Find someone who *believes* in your strengths, acknowledges your flaws, and can still offer *encouragement* and *support* because they *trust* you to tap into the resilient core that has sustained you in the past. My respected friend John Alston says, "A friend is someone who opens a window and lets the sun shine into a dark room."

You can't overestimate the value of having a strong personal support system. As the angel tells Jimmy Stewart in Frank Capra's film *It's a Wonderful Life*, "No man is a failure who has friends." One characteristic of the unresilient that I've observed is their difficulty in sustaining friendships. I don't know whether this is a cause of nonresilience or a consequence. It's a chicken-egg dilemma. Either way, if you find yourself feeling less than resilient, firmly resist the temptation to retreat and cut yourself off from others. Instead, set a goal of cultivating positive, supportive relationships in your life.

Make a mental list headed "Friends." Ask yourself, "Who would stick with me if I suffered major setbacks? Who could I count on through thick and thin, even if I weren't in a position to do them favors?" These people are your *real* friends! If your list is a short one and you want to expand it, start a second list headed, "Who can count on my unfailing love and friendship?" When you expand list #2, you'll expand list #1.

BOUNCE HIGHER TIP

If you want to have strong, nurturing friends
who lift you up,
start by being such a friend.

The Dance of Love

When Charlie Wedemeyer was thirty, he had a life many would envy. He had been an award-winning football player at Punahoe High School in Hawaii and an outstanding college player at Michigan State University. He went on to become a successful high school teacher and football coach at Los Gatos High School in California, married a beautiful woman, Lucy, and was blessed with two gorgeous children, daughter Carri and son Kale.

One day Charlie noticed that he was having trouble gripping the chalk when he wrote on the blackboard. Then his whole right arm grew weak. The family physician suggested a battery of tests. The diagnosis was worse than anything they could have imagined:

ALS/Lou Gehrig's disease. "Charlie, you have two years to live," the doctor told him.

That was nineteen years ago. As I write this, Charlie is still very much alive. Certainly ALS has wreaked havoc with his body. He has lost the use of his limbs, the ability to raise his head, and he can no longer talk. A respirator gives him oxygen and a feeding tube provides the nourishment to keep him alive. What ALS has taken from the Wedemeyer family is obvious. But it has also revealed their resilience.

Charlie told me that he doesn't want anyone's sympathy. "Roger, remember that we're *all* terminal. I've already outlived one of my doctors. I've got ALS. My wife's got PMS. We've all got something. What I found out nineteen years ago was that ALS was my diagnosis, but misery was strictly optional."

"Hold on," you may be muttering, "I thought you said that Charlie Wedemeyer couldn't talk." That's right. He can't. However, he and his wife, Lucy, have improvised their own communication strategy. As Lucy concentrates intensely on Charlie's face, he begins to blink his eyes and move his lips slightly. He has limited use of his facial muscles, so they have developed a lip-reading shorthand system. A more accurate description would be "face reading." Lucy says, "Many spouses go weeks without looking into each other's eyes, but we do it on an hourly basis." Watching them communicate is one of the most inspiring experiences I've had. Quite often during the marriage ceremony, you hear the words "these two will be as one," but the Wedemeyers have captured this ideal more than any couple I know. They communicate so beautifully and effortlessly that you are mesmerized. It's like watching two marvelous dancers who know each other's moves instinctively.

When thirty-year-old Charlie told his wife that she would soon be a widow with two young children, he was overcome with emotion. Lucy replied that this wasn't his disease, it was *their* disease. They would fight it together.

Some people might mistakenly believe that their relationship is no longer one of equal give and take, that Lucy is now doing all the giving and Charlie all the taking. Lucy is the first to put that notion to rest. "It bothers me," she says, "when people think I'm some kind of self-sacrificing Florence Nightingale who gets nothing out of the relationship. Charlie is a constant source of support, more so than in many marriages. Whenever there are moments that I feel I can't handle, I just look at my sweet, handsome husband and he gives me a wink or a smile or he says 'I love you' and my strength returns."

Charlie and Lucy have developed a keen appreciation of the ridiculous and unexpected. Lucy tells one story about her real-estate business, which requires her to drive clients around to look at properties. When Charlie lost control of his neck muscles, she got in the habit of putting out her hand to keep his head from whiplashing when she made a turn or sudden stop. The habit became so automatic that she sometimes found herself grabbing the forehead of a very startled client.

The children have responded creatively to the problems of decreased mobility. When Lucy's job made it hard for her to drive Charlie to his job as high school coach, daughter Carri transferred to a nearby school so she could run him over to the football field in a golf cart. Both children have been constantly inventive in finding solutions as new problems arise.

What all the Wedemeyers have taught me reaffirms my belief in the resilience-building power of human relationships. Because of their positive attitudes and unwavering faith in one another, they are leading full and vibrant lives. They are truly hungry for what no one can take from them—respect, caring, kindness, intimacy, and genuine friendship. As we parted, Charlie said, "I hope the Crawfords and the Wedemeyers will be lifelong friends."

I asked Charlie what he missed most. "Hugging," he replied. "Being able to put my arms around someone and give them a hug. But I still *get* plenty of hugs. ALS can take everything from me except what I need most—love and laughter."

Loyalty Repaid

Even before the ashes had cooled after a devastating fire, help began to pour in for the Nutmeg Chrome Company. First, President William Logozzo met with employees, forging a mutual commitment to rebuild the forty-four-year-old West Hartford, Connecticut, metal-finishing firm. Then former employees, neighboring businesses, and even competitors pledged their help. Temporary offices were set up in a neighbor's building, and competitors allowed Nutmeg employees to use their premises and plating equipment at night and on weekends.

Employees were included in the decision making, and their ideas were actively solicited. New safety and efficiency features were designed into the new plant. Employees celebrated as each stage of the recovery was completed. Meanwhile, customers were kept informed, and most continued to send work to the temporary facilities. Sales have increased every year since. "We couldn't have rebuilt this place without everyone's help," says Logozzo. "It's comforting to know that we have friends like these."

In the business world, friendship translates as loyalty rather than intimacy. Businesses that stand by clients, employees, and suppliers are the ones most likely to have their loyalty and support. In *The Platinum Rule*, Dr. Tony Alessandra advises that we "do unto others as they'd like to be done unto." You can't beat this philosophy for building the loyalty necessary for resilient organizations. During the inevitable crises and business downturns, such support is an extra resource for resilient survival.

Build Your Foundation

Ask yourself the same questions about your work relationships that you did about your private life. "Who is important to me?" Make a list. Now imagine that each of these people has experienced a major loss—their job, home, or spouse, even their reputation. How would you react? Would you still be a friend? Would the relationship as it now exists survive such an ordeal? Would your friendship continue to grow and deepen with new, shared experiences? Or would you quickly exhaust the past as a source of conversation?

Look through the other end of the telescope. Who would come to visit you if you were flat on your back, useless as a wage earner, service provider, or business contact? Have you established bonds of love and friendship that go beyond convenience and proximity?

Set aside one day simply to notice the goodness in others. If someone does something that would usually bring a complaint to your lips or resentment to your heart, instead feel a rush of pleasure because you can now recognize how relatively trivial this action really is. At the end of this day, I'll bet you'll have noticed that you feel better about others, others feel better about you, and you feel better about yourself.

Usually the hardest time to overlook and sympathize with other people's faults is when our own are under attack and our resilience is low. It can feel like a fight for survival. One thing quickly leads to another, and you can easily find yourself locked in a cycle of destructive recriminations and ill feeling. That's why it's important to step back and ask yourself what is most important to you? What is your bottom line? Once you have this mental list, then everything else is a foible, perhaps charming, perhaps irritating, but something that you are resilient enough to accommodate. (In the 1989 film *When Harry Met Sally*, Harry realizes he loves Sally when he can honestly say of her most irritating traits, "I *love* that you get cold when it's seventy-one degrees out. I *love* that it takes you an hour and a half to order a sandwich . . .")

Many of us have enormous responsibilities and crushing sched ules, so the time for building relationships becomes doubly precious. We stay hungry when we remember that we are constantly giving and getting from others, not physical things, but enormous gifts of joy, patience, understanding, compassion, wisdom, and loyalty.

PROFILE

Richard Santana

Many people make remarkable journeys, but find it hard to pinpoint the exact factors that contributed to their resilience. That's why it was so exciting for me to talk to Richard Santana, an articulate man who has thought about the catalysts that helped him swap a life of drugs and crime for a career in education.

Deserted by his father before birth, orphaned three months later when his mother died, he spent his childhood in a succession of foster homes in Fresno, California, until he was nine. Then his maternal aunt obtained custody, and Richard's life seemed about to change. It did, but not for the better.

His well-meaning aunt had an ex-con boyfriend who was a gang member. This man became young Richard's male role model, and the nine-year-old's involvement with gangs and drugs began. Richard admired his "uncle" for his aggressiveness, affluence, and seeming invincibility. While other men in the neighborhood toiled at menial, minimum-wage jobs and faced frequent unemployment, "Uncle" maintained a comfortable lifestyle by selling drugs. Uncle seemed to know all the answers, and Richard was a fast learner. Within a year, Richard was accepted as a full-fledged gang member, involved in drug deals and other criminal activities. His gang name was "Mr. Chah-Ko-La-Tay" because of his dark Latino complexion.

By the ninth grade, Richard had moved out of his aunt's home and been suspended from school. He lived with other gang members in a house rented with drug profits. But even with all this acceptance and surface "success," Richard remained a bitter, angry young man. "I was desperately looking for someone to love me," he told me.

Then he and some friends were shot at by a rival gang.

This was the first turning point for Richard. Usually such incidents set off a cycle of gang retaliation that can take many lives. But instead of craving revenge, Richard started to think: "I never had a father. When I was young, seven or eight, I used to see kids playing with their fathers, and it made me terribly angry. They had something I didn't. Now, many of my older friends had children, but they were killing each other and leaving those children without fathers. I realized that if anything was going to change, I had to start by changing my life."

His immediate goal became clear. Go back to school. To overturn his suspension, he asked the Chicano Youth Center to plead his case with the District Review Board. They did and he was reinstated. One condition was that he had to get involved in school activities, and Richard was assigned the job of selling advertisements for the school yearbook. He told me he applied his sales experience to persuading businesses to buy ads. He added with a chuckle, "I wore the only clothes I had. When I walked in wearing gang attire, I quickly got their attention." He sold $2,500 in ads, far surpassing any other salesperson.

School triggered another turning point in Richard's life. His class reading assignments included two books "that would change my life forever." One was J. D. Salinger's *The Catcher in the Rye*, the classic story of a teenager in emotional turmoil. Richard identified with the pain and struggles of Holden Caulfield, and realized that, though they came from very different backgrounds, they experienced similar conflicts. The other influential book was a biography of Martin Luther King Jr. "Dr. King taught me the value of civility, kindness, and rising above your circumstances." Richard became a voracious reader, increasing his knowledge and, in turn, his self-image. Before, a high point in his life had been showing off a pair of expensive new shoes bought with drug money. Now, it was earning a diploma from Fresno's Roosevelt School, a scholarship to Fresno State—and, eventually, a master's degree in education from Harvard.

Today, Richard works with high-risk young people involved with gangs. What he teaches them is that education is the only deterrent to gangs. "When I was a gang member," says Richard, "I thought that power meant having a gun. Now I know that power means having knowledge, both about myself and the world. That's the core of my resilience."

RESILIENCE BUILDER

Stay Hungry for Knowledge, Friendship, and Adventure

1. Seek Knowledge

Identify something you'd like to learn and also something you feel you *should* learn. Make a contract with yourself to start this week. If the "should-know" category is labor-intensive or unpleasant, consider rewarding yourself by alternating the difficult and pleasurable learning sessions.

2. Build Friendships

- Name five people who are important to you. How do you maintain and deepen your friendship? Do you sometimes do things that could weaken the friendship?
- What new friends have you made in the last two years? What is the basis of your friendship?
- Describe five things you've done in the past twenty-four hours that demonstrate your respect for others.
- What can you *do* (not buy) in the next twenty-four hours to show someone you care?

3. Stretch Yourself

- What was the last challenge that you decided not to confront? Reevaluate your decision. Did you have sound reasons or were you just trying to avoid discomfort or possible failure?
- Are you good at spotting opportunities, saying things like "Boy, what a terrific idea," or "Why can't they . . . ?" List at least three of these ideas. Then describe what motivations, skills, talents, and expertise would be needed

to carry out your great ideas. Can you imagine interesting others in the ideas?

- Write a paragraph or more about your last three "adventures." (You'll be surprised what you learn about yourself.)

Coffee Talk

A mature gentleman approached me after one of my talks. I'm always hungry for feedback, and, since he had an enthusiastic smile, I was especially eager for his input. "Roger," he said, "hearing you speak today completely changed my thinking about my own ability to be resilient. Now I'm sure that I'll be able to overcome any adversity that comes along. Halfway through your presentation, you said something that I desperately needed to hear."

A warm feeling of self-importance swept over me. What a master motivator I am! Through my eloquence and insights, this man had made a major change in his self-image. "Yes, Roger," he continued, "before your talk, I drank four cups of coffee. Thirty minutes later, I had to go. Then you said, 'the foundation of resilience is believing success is possible.' That inspired me. I began telling myself, 'I can hold it! I can hold it!' And I made it through your entire presentation!"

5

Use All Your Resources

Eleven days after a terrible earthquake in Russia, a mother and her infant were pulled alive from the rubble. Mother Teresa was among those who came to nurse the survivors. As she walked through a hospital, she came upon the woman, badly crushed and near death, with a healthy baby lying beside her. Puzzled at the difference in their condition, Mother Teresa asked the nurses if this was the child's mother. Yes, she was assured. They had both been trapped when their building collapsed. Without food or water to sustain her, the mother's breast milk had ceased to flow, but she had kept the baby alive by slicing her finger and squeezing her blood into the child's mouth.

Most of us never realize the incredible strengths we have until we are tested. We also rarely recognize how much we know and how many resources we have, both inside and outside ourselves, until they are called on. Some of our resources, like knowledge and ability, are more apparent. Some are intangible but priceless, like the love, trust, faith, and respect of others. And others are conscientious deposits in our resilience accounts. Recognizing your enormous reservoir of personal strengths and assets can pay unexpected dividends in difficult times.

Resource #1—Your Talents and Skills

Some people think that if you just do something long enough and hard enough, you have to succeed. They take a special pride in "pushing the envelope" as they strive in areas that are awkward and unpleasant for them. This may be an admirable philosophy, but it can also be a trap. Too many people waste their time trying to improve what they do badly at the expense of what they do well.

Resilient people go toward their strengths and learn how to compensate for their weaknesses. They focus on the talents they have, and not on those they lack. Resilient people concentrate on what they do right, nonresilient people on what they do wrong. Why struggle to achieve mediocrity at something because the discomfort is "good for you"?

BOUNCE HIGHER TIP

*Don't let what you can't do
get in the way of what you can do.*

Start by deciding what you're really good at. This can be more difficult if you have labeled yourself with a job description and can't see beyond the title to your true skills and resources. Abandon limiting labels like "podiatrist" or "mother of three" or "lab technician," and pretend that you're being quizzed by a wise ré-sumé consultant about your real aptitudes and attitudes.

- Are you best at the big picture?
- Or great at details?
- Do you relish working alone?
- Or do you especially enjoy working with people?
- Are you strongly responsive to your environment?
- Or are you usually so wrapped up in what you're doing that a brass band could march through the room without your noticing?

Each and every one of these contradictory skills offers a valu-able clue to your true resources. Whenever you run into road-blocks, an inventory of your distinctive abilities will suggest new directions.

I met a young woman on a plane who told me she had trained as a chef and was working her way up in the restaurant business when she developed carpal tunnel syndrome. She could no longer lift heavy skillets and chop vegetables. She went to a career coun-selor who helped her discover that the aspect of cooking that she enjoyed most was making fancy pastries, a job that required a strong aesthetic sense, attention to detail, and patience. After spe-cial training, she has started over as an art restorer, a career that de-mands and utilizes those exact qualities to the fullest.

Learn to see *all* your many talents, skills, and intelligences. Yes, "intelligences" should be plural. If you're still haunted by that D in algebra, a low SAT score, or not being able to afford college, you need a fresh perspective: Everything you do, every day, reflects your level of "intelligence" in a specified area. Harvard psycholo-gist Howard Gardner estimates that we have at least seven com-plex forms of intelligence, not just the verbal and math skills tested on standard IQ tests.

1. Interpersonal—your ability to understand others' moods and concerns.

2. Introspective—your ability to understand yourself, your own feelings, abilities, and needs.

3. Spatial—your ability to perceive visual shapes, locations, movement, and dimensions.

4. Bodily—your consciousness and control of your body, your motor skills.

5. Musical—your skill at distinguishing and re-creating tones and rhythms.

6. Verbal—how you process language, both spoken and written.

7. Math or logical—your ability to sequence and evaluate information.

How intelligent are you? Before you can answer, you need to ask, "Which of my many kinds of intelligence?" In fact, some researchers estimate that we have more than fifty different kinds, each translating into many different skills.

Intelligence, of course, isn't knowledge. And knowledge isn't always knowing the answer. It's knowing where and how to find the answer. Real education, the kind that resilient people seek, gives guidelines for gathering and evaluating information. Where do you go when you need facts and advice? Because you are flexible (Chapter 2) and hungry (Chapter 4), your list of resources is constantly expanding!

Recognizing our own skills and talents isn't always easy. Back in Chapter 1, "Believe Success Is Possible," you saw how resilient and nonresilient people look at positive and negative events through different ends of the telescope. The same is true about judging our own characteristics. Resilient people think that their best qualities are rare and precious, while their faults are common and ordinary. Nonresilient people believe just the opposite. They think that everyone else possesses the same good qualities, while their own faults are rare and grievous.

High resilience requires stopping to notice your strengths, evident and not so evident. You'll find more take-stock questions in the "Resilience Builder" section of this chapter. Don't be timid.

Any accountant will tell you that it's not vanity to have a realistic inventory of your assets. Your unique combination of skills and limitations makes you different from everyone else on earth. Respect and celebrate that uniqueness.

Resource #2—Your Limitations

I was fascinated to find out that the word *handicap* comes from an old horse-racing term. Just before a race, each jockey would put his hand in the starter's cap to draw a post position. When horses run on an oval track, the horse nearest the center has the advantage of a shorter distance to travel. The outer jockeys have drawn less-advantageous positions from their "hand in cap." We all draw different post positions in life, but the horse next to the rail isn't always the winner.

We are all born with some limitations—physical, emotional, or intellectual. Some are easily seen, some aren't. Never confuse your inborn limitations with the weaknesses you can actually change, like procrastination, pessimism, or anger.

Most people concentrate on using their strengths, but to be truly resilient we also need to acknowledge and use our flaws. Often we can find real inspiration in some limitation. The sculptor creates a masterpiece from a flawed block of marble. The scientist finds a major discovery in something discarded from a failed experiment. Two team members each provide the strengths and skills the other lacks.

If you identify a real shortcoming, ask yourself:

- How can I overcome this limitation? Is it worth the effort?
- How can I use this limitation? (For example, someone with dyslexia might use insights gained from this challenge to develop a new system for teaching reading.)
- How can I compensate for this limitation? (Someone with dyslexia might find a business partner to handle the reading and written records, then concentrate on the part of the job that he or she is really good at.)

These questions focus you on your personal growth, not on repairing perceived deficiencies. They are enormously valuable, because they also let you know what isn't going to work.

Some people fear that revealing their limitations will devalue their strengths. But when you are honest about your limitations, you draw people to you.

Be curious about your limitations and what they can teach you. Then you'll be able to identify your true strengths.

Resource #3—Role Models

A role model is a great external source of resilience. Everyone starts life by modeling the behavior they see around them, good or bad. As they mature, resilient people consciously choose role models who have the qualities and skills they admire and want to emulate. No other form of education is so cheap and painless.

The Reverend Michael Pyburn shared a great story with me about the power of modeling. It concerns funny money. Today almost anyone with a larcenous nature and a good photocopy machine can turn out passable counterfeit money. That's why the Secret Service has stepped up its counterfeit-identification training until new antifraud technologies are in place. The old identification method was to have agents study counterfeit bills, seeing what was wrong with them. The new technique is to have them study real money. They feel it, they fold it, they examine every detail. They imprint the real thing on their consciousness. Then when they run across a phony, they know almost instinctively that something isn't right.

You can use positive role models the same way. Study the real thing—high-functioning achievers and resilient optimists. You can actually train your instincts to lead you in the direction you want to go.

Make sure you use your role models to lift yourself up, not put yourself down. Beware of the negative-comparison game. Remember when you were a kid and someone said, "Why can't you be more like so-and-so?" How did that make you feel? Probably rotten. Chances are that didn't motivate you to do better. Such negative comparisons don't work any better for adults—even when the voice telling you to shape up is your own.

So what can you do when you feel some twinges of envy, resentment, or inadequacy along with admiration? Whenever this happens, stop, take a deep breath, and ask yourself, "What can I learn from this person?"

For example, a newly appointed vice president was distressed that her ideas and suggestions seemed to be ignored at meetings. She could easily have blamed sex discrimination or personal inadequacy, but she decided instead to find a role model. There was another vice president who was always listened to. Instead of envying him, she carefully watched what he did, and she discovered her key mistake. Like most people, she had been presenting her ideas in a more-is-better style, starting with background and going through her thought processes to an end result. However, her role model reversed the process. He started with the bottom line, providing details and background only when asked. Also, he never argued when others resisted his ideas. Instead, he asked them questions, showing he was genuinely interested in their concerns. He'd figured out, perhaps through trial and error, that this was the best way to work with this particular group. When the new vice president adopted his strategy, her colleagues suddenly started listening to her.

BOUNCE HIGHER TIP

When you notice that other people's actions lead to positive outcomes, you can decide that "I can do that too."

Mentors, instructors, and coaches can be role models. Until recently, it was customary to serve a formal apprenticeship to learn a craft or skill. The master directed and supervised the development of the novice. Today, mentors are more informal, but no less valuable. Do you look for the right people to advise you about what you want to know and do? Have you figured out how to approach them so that they feel honored by your confidence and are eager to help you? When you get help from others, do you demonstrate by your growth and integrity that you deserved it? And do you express your gratitude, if not with words, then with your deeds?

You may never be able to thank your role models face-to-face, but you still do so in spirit every time you draw strength from their examples and inspiration from their lives. This is their immortality . . . and yours.

Resource #4—Your Cheering Section

The great therapist Dr. Virginia Satir once told me that when she walked into a post office, she always scanned the faces on the Wanted posters to see if she recognized any of them. "Roger, you know why all these people are 'Wanted,' don't you?" she asked.

"No, why?" I said.

"Because they don't *feel* wanted," she replied. The greatest need that we have as human beings is to be validated and affirmed.

Identify your support group. Your boosters, supporters, champions, and cheerleaders may also be your role models and mentors, but they don't have to be. They can be your kids, the guy who sells you your morning cup of coffee, someone in your exercise class, even your dog. We all need a cheering section to celebrate our successes and sustain us through our failures. Not faultfinders ("Boy, you really blew it.") and not self-appointed victims looking for company ("They sure have it in for people like us.") You need people who'll remind you that setbacks are temporary and you're capable of hanging on and pulling ahead.

Marty Rodriguez is a phenomenal success in an occupation that requires resilience on an hourly basis. She is a sales professional.

Marty is one of the top Realtors in the world, selling over fifty million dollars' worth of California property annually. I had heard about her incredible achievements for some time, so, when we finally met, I couldn't wait to ask, *"What sustains your resilience?"*

"Salespeople are acknowledged for individual achievement," she told me, "but no one ever does it alone." Marty has surrounded herself with what she calls her Dream Team, a cheering section that includes her husband, brother, son, daughter, and niece. "Each of us has particular strengths to meet different challenges, and I have friends and family I can go to anytime for advice. They've all helped me recognize and develop my special gifts and talents."

When I asked Marty, "Where are you coming from?" she told me about growing up one of eleven children in a two-bedroom home. Her family wasn't rich, she says, but they possessed vast inner wealth. "My parents showed us the importance of work. My mother taught us that people judge you by what you can do, not where you come from, and my father showed us how to create our own environment of achievement. He was a great success coach."

BOUNCE HIGHER TIP

Start recruiting your Dream Team today.

Who is your success coach? Everyone needs one, even Michael Jordan. The gift these coaches give us is refusing to accept anything but our best effort. There are times you may stop believing in yourself, but great coaches never do.

That's what every successful manager, parent, and teacher has in common—a deep, unwavering belief in the potential of others, and the ability to convey this confidence and excitement. We all need these personal success coaches in our lives, people whose expectations for us are higher than those we can imagine for ourselves on a really good day. Not too high, or we reject them as impossible and stop trying. Not too low, or we have no challenges. It's that "just right" factor that defines the truly great boosters.

Once my wife and I were shopping in a Louisiana department store. Donna was in the dress department and I was looking at men's suits. They had size 42-regular and 42-long, but of course they didn't have my size, which is 42-weird. A salesman approached and asked if he could be of assistance. I explained that it would take too many alterations to make any of the suits fit me.

"Most athletic men have that problem," he replied. I turned and started to walk away, then stopped.

"Would you say that again, please?"

"Most athletic men have that problem," he repeated. What a discerning expert! I tried on the suit. It fit pretty well. The arms and legs were long, but they could be altered. I then asked, "Is this the type of suit an athletic man like me should be wearing?"

"Yes, sir, and there are several others here on the rack that you should have as well." It was a rather expensive day.

As I waited by the cash register, I noticed a small sign intended for the eyes of the sales staff. "Don't neglect the lagniappe," it said. I asked what that meant. He explained that *lagniappe* (pronounced LAN-yap) was a common word in Cajun country, meaning "beyond full measure," something like a baker's dozen. It's like getting free delivery or throwing in a set of jumper cables. That's the lagniappe. We can all use some verbal lagniappe and ego strokes in our everyday encounters. Give them whenever you can, and be sure to recognize and relish them when they come your way. Appreciate your onetime boosters as well as the ongoing ones.

Does it seem like a weakness to need positive feedback from others? Shouldn't we be so secure that we're immune from outside opinions? Hardly. Responding realistically to the expectations of others is one of the components of self-esteem.

As a speaker, I'm always looking for ways to improve how I get my message across. When I started out, I set out those standard evaluation sheets with boxes to check for excellent, good, fair, poor, and then a space for comments and suggestions. I quickly found that most people just checked a box and left the suggestion area blank, leaving me with no clues on how I could improve.

Then one day a bright young lady approached me, clutching a notebook. "Roger, I've just listened to you for ninety minutes," she said, "and I've taken fifteen pages of notes." She began making comments, referring to the notebook. Suddenly, I had a brainstorm. I asked if she'd be willing to send me photocopies of her notes. A week later, they arrived. Those notes taught me more about how people processed my information than all the evaluation sheets I had reviewed over the years. I learned what she thought was important enough to write down, how she had interpreted it, and, even more valuable, what she hadn't bothered to take notes about. She showed me what I needed to clarify and what I was already doing right.

Now, when people stop to talk with me after my speeches, I ask them if they'd let me have a copy of their notes. So far no one has been reluctant, even though what they wrote was intended just for their own use. Usually they feel flattered that I value their input. The notes I get offer immediate feedback, showing me what's working and what's not. My audiences are educating me as much as I am educating them.

Resource #5—Your Imagination

Imagination may seem an unusual tool for increasing resilience, but it's essential. We build our resilient self by rehearsing with conscious images. This includes active and constructive daydreaming.

Remember back to your childhood when you visualized yourself as a prima ballerina in front of the mirror? Or as a president? Encourage yourself to daydream like this as an adult. One of my childhood heroes was the great Los Angeles Lakers guard Jerry West. In our backyard I would visualize myself with five seconds left in the game, dribbling the ball to the top of the key and letting it fly, then hearing the crowd cheer wildly as my shot dropped perfectly through the center of the hoop with a swish. As I grew older, the basketballs were replaced by tennis balls.

All of us daydream like this when we're kids. Then, as we get older, most of us become terminally "mature" and decide we must "be serious." We lose a powerful resource, one we should use all our lives.

We can call on our imagination to program our minds to assure a positive outcome. There are a variety of terms for this process: *mental rehearsal, mental imaging, positive imaging, visualization,* and *scripting.* They all describe the same powerful inner reality.

Mental rehearsal is far more than just wishing something would happen. It begins with making positive mental pictures of what we want to do and be. This can be a specific task we want our body to do, or it can be the role and goals we want to achieve. Psychologists tell us that each time we have an experience, positive or negative, it is recorded by both body and mind. Have you ever recalled a frightening or exciting experience and found that your heart was beating more rapidly? Have you ever thought of a loved one and felt calmer, or thought about dinner and started salivating? What about harnessing those same mental powers to your conscious planning process?

The potential of imaging is especially powerful in sports. Golfer Tiger Woods tells how he never hits a shot without first clearly visualizing a flawlessly executed swing, the ball's perfect flight, and then its precision landing on the green. A successful shot, Tiger Woods says, is 50 percent visualization, 40 percent setup, and only 10 percent swing. Outstanding pro athletes like Steve Young describe visualizing or *imaging* each of their plays again and again before a game. Many world-class athletes feel their success is closely related to the vividness of their mental practice. Effective visualization isn't limited to sports. It has proven equally useful for job interviews, sales calls, and board meetings.

As we've already seen, resilient people teach themselves to build on the past, both positive and negative. They consciously draw energy, endurance, and inspiration from their achievements and experiences to create positive expectations for the future. Then they use their imaginations to visualize an upcoming opportunity so vividly that it seems to be happening in the present.

How to Use Mental Rehearsal

Find a comfortable, peaceful place. Start by breathing deeply and clearing your mind of your current thoughts. Imagine that your mind is a blackboard covered with writing. Then erase it.

Next, think of an upcoming event that is important to you. As you do this, keep a positive image of yourself experiencing the event and responding competently and coolly. See yourself shaping and dictating the outcome. Look out through your own eyes and experience your body performing. If you catch yourself feeling anxious or anticipating a negative outcome, pause and recall a time when you handled a difficult situation well and the good feelings you experienced. Then resume your enactment of this coming event. Once you've walked through your ideal scenario, go back and anticipate any possible roadblocks. Then solve them, anticipating positive outcomes.

These positive imagining exercises can and do produce positive real-life results, enhancing your ability to handle challenging events when they actually occur. Think of them as mental fire drills. Your mental rehearsal lets you enjoy the actual experience because you feel prepared. You'll be more confident and better able to roll with the inevitable punches that life throws at us.

BOUNCE HIGHER TIP

*You are both playwright and star
of your life script.
You can change the characters and scenes,
and even rewrite the ending!*

Resource #6—Self-Acceptance

As human beings, we seem never to be quite satisfied with ourselves. If we have curly hair, we wish it were straight. It it's straight, we admire other people's curls. Perhaps some body part seems "too large" or "too small." We covet others' physical attributes, even if they were created by a photo retoucher with an airbrush.

I've experienced this in my own life. My hands and legs were not just somewhat different from those of most people, they were drastically different. As a child, I would sometimes dream that I would wake up magically transformed. Then I reached my teens and acquired the requisite teen mania for dressing, talking, and behaving exactly like all my friends. Along with yearning to fit in with the right clothes and slang and attitudes, I yearned for something everyone else had. I wanted to have hands.

A physician came up with what I thought was a wonderful solution: a pair of artificial hands. They wouldn't increase my dexterity, but they would look more like the real thing. Now my life was going to change drastically. I would be able to walk through a shopping mall or go to a restaurant and nobody would stare. They would never suspect that I was different. I could hardly wait.

My new hands arrived. They were a work of art. Made of a rubberlike substance, they slipped over my existing hands like gloves. I remember putting them on for the first time. I stared at the long slender fingers, the beautiful fingernails. They were perfect, everything I had dreamed of. As I walked toward a three-way mirror, I almost didn't recognize myself. Not only had my hands changed, but the expression on my face had changed too. Boy, had my life improved. I'd even be able to wear the school ring.

You may be thinking that this was an incredible turning point in my life. You're right. It was, but not the way you imagine. I wore those hands for just one day. Then I recognized that, when I put them on, I felt I was being dishonest with myself. It was like trying to hide who I really was. So I took off those handsome artificial hands and have never worn them since.

The life-altering change in me was inside. I realized that, no matter how resilient my attitude is or how great my optimism and vision, my hands and my legs will forever be the way they are. I can't change them. The moment I accepted this, I was free to focus on everything that was *right* about my life.

Reinhold Niebuhr's famous prayer exemplifies the resilient attitude: "Give me the courage to change what should be changed, the serenity to accept what cannot be changed, and the wisdom to know the difference."

Self-acceptance offers a surprise bonus: It improves how we feel about other people. If you've decided you're a worthwhile person, you tend to see others the same way, despite their foibles and weaknesses. Yes, there's a lot of less-than-acceptable behavior out there, but people with strong self-images are usually slow to offer criticism and negative judgments. They recognize that constant faultfinding erodes their own sense of self-worth. If we can't accept anything less than perfection in others, we will inevitably fall short of our own unrealistic standards.

Mark Twain said that everyone is a moon with a side we never see. When someone fails to meet your expectations, try to imagine that hidden side. Instead of easy labels like "two-faced," "arrogant," "incompetent," or "rude," use resilient language like "confused," "shy," "still learning," or "distracted." When we're kind to others, we're really being kind to ourselves.

Resource #7—A Healthy Body

Many people in poor health are remarkably resilient, but the truth is that a healthy, cared-for body gives an extra bounce to everything we do. When we don't get enough sleep or exercise or we overindulge or forget to eat, we can weaken our ability to fight both viruses and vicissitudes. Even something as simple as a hot shower or a haircut can restore the sense of physical well-being essential to resilience. If you're in the midst of a difficult challenge, taking care of yourself is essential.

When I participated in high school and collegiate sports, I

constantly reconfirmed the mind-body connection. I learned that any time you're feeling unresilient, physical activity can provide a quick fix. That's because *motion affects emotion*. It's harder to feel discouraged when you are walking, jogging, or playing. Regular exercise is a solid defense against nonresilience.

There's a scientific reason for this. According to physiologists, physical activity increases the body's production of natural mood lifters called endorphins. Endorphins are morphine-like chemicals that renew and fortify us, even promoting restful sleep. When you're feeling "up" and positive and rested, you're ready to be at your most resilient. And, as a bonus, you're going to look better. That's another self-image enhancement.

If you're already involved in a regular fitness program, keep at it. If you haven't kept up this valuable mood elevator (or if you haven't started), now's the time to get your resilience-building endorphins pounding.

Choose an activity. Biking, jogging, or aerobics are fine, but just walking will do. Start slowly and increase gradually. Consistency and endurance are the key. The message is simple. The next time you ask yourself, "How long have I been there?" perhaps one answer is, "Too long on the couch." If you want to improve your resilience, self-esteem, and health, get moving!

Resource #8—Hope

Hope is intensely personal, yet we can't maintain it without a profound sense of interconnectedness, of being part of something bigger than ourselves. That's because hope isn't just believing that things will get better for *you*. Even people facing death can maintain hope if they believe that things will get better for *others*.

Hope is the energizer for everything we attempt, a constantly renewable source of resilience. It is also the ultimate tool for coping with uncertainty, suffering, and loss.

Psychologists and philosophers have long recognized that people can learn to be helpless and hopeless, but here's terrific news: If we can learn to be hopeless, we can also learn *hopefulness*.

There are two main strategies for maintaining hope in the face of difficulties:

- Change the situation.
- Change how you feel about the situation.

When people are feeling especially resilient, they try to change things. When they're not or when change is difficult, they concentrate on managing their own emotions. The most successful strategy is to combine both approaches. So use all your resources: Back up your positive attitude by figuring out practical ways to solve, eliminate, or go around the problem.

But some challenges in life are unavoidable. Aging, for one, and often the elderly have valuable lessons to teach us all. Asked to define *hope*, elderly people have suggested that it is "a sense of aliveness and inner strength." But when asked what threatened their hope levels, many listed "hopelessness in others." If hopelessness can be catching, hopefulness should be catching too!

How can you "catch" hope? Using the framework of this book, here are some time-honored strategies:

Where Are You Coming From?

- **Uplifting memories.** Build on your positive past.
- **Lightheartedness.** Make a special effort to tap your sense of delight and the playfulness of your inner spirit.
- **Positive images.** At difficult times, focus on a specific object or image from the past that inspires hope; for example, a gift or message from a friend, or a song lyric.

How Long Have You Been There?

- **Interconnectedness.** See yourself as a crucial part of a huge, interdependent network connecting you with others and the world.

- **Spiritual beliefs and practices.** See a larger purpose in the events that are troubling you.
- **Positive self-talk.** Talk to yourself in positive terms, envisioning hoped-for outcomes.

Where Are You Going?

- **Purposeful activities.** Keep active at working toward meaningful goals.
- **Reinterpretation.** Identify an exciting challenge that may be hiding in the difficulties you face.
- **Anticipation.** Look forward to something pleasant in the future.

Above all, cultivate a "great expectation of good." I first heard this phrase used to describe the delightful British comedian Joyce Grenfell. A few days before her death from a brain tumor, Grenfell called a friend to say she had wonderful news. She had been concerned about how her beloved husband, Reggie, would get by without her, but now she was elated. "Reggie has suddenly learned to cook, so there's nothing to worry about at all!"

Resource #9—Faith and Prayer

There are many things worth believing that we cannot see, and even more that can never be seen unless we choose to believe in them. These include faith in the goodness of others, faith in our own abilities, faith that a task is worth doing, that love is worth risking, and that life is worth living. Faith is how we interpret the world to ourselves, and how we interpret our place in it.

For those who acknowledge God or a higher power, prayer is a way to strengthen faith by putting it into words. Prayer can serve as a simple acknowledgment of the day and the moment, refreshing us like a drink of cool water. In difficult times, it can provide hour-by-hour renewal.

For the resilient, faith is an inescapable, everyday necessity. Faith lets us describe life in strongly positive terms, which is the hallmark of resilience. Even a prayer for strength and resilience shows that we have faith that we can and will find internal resources in order to triumph. Whenever you tell yourself, "I can't take this any longer!" you're internalizing the image of yourself as weak and unable to cope. But when you pray for strength, you're creating a picture of yourself as able to achieve and overcome. Through prayer, you deepen faith and belief in your own abilities. The greater your faith, the greater your possibilities in life.

Sooner or later, we all face times when we have to rely on resilience alone to keep us going. Unresilient people usually wait until this moment to start praying. They see the power of prayer as a last resort. (I've often observed this on turbulent flights, where visible praying increases in direct ratio to the severity of the bumps.) Resilient people, however, stop frequently to notice and be grateful for the good things around them. This increases their overall sense that life is supporting them. One of my favorite prayers is by industrialist Henry J. Kaiser:

Oh, God, keep me on the path of achieving happiness and success that are real. Keep my vision always clear. Help me to practice faith—faith in God, faith in my fellow man, and faith in my own best self. Help me to tap the hidden powers within and above me. Give me strength to work with all the energies of mind and body. Help me to practice the love of people and service to others. Keep me forever with a smile on my face for the whole human race.

In these few words, Kaiser summarizes the resilient life. I believe that God gives us all the life-quality of resilience. How we choose to cultivate and use it is up to us.

PROFILE

Deirdre Stanford

She was articulate, accomplished, poised, and a commanding communicator. Most people were unaware that Deirdre Hamilton Stanford was unable to speak a complete sentence until she was ten years old.

Deirdre was born profoundly deaf. Her parents were told she would have severe learning difficulties and never lead an independent life. Instead, she grew up to earn a master's degree in clinical psychology and become a college instructor.

Deirdre had combined brains with beauty when she entered the Miss California Pageant, the first hearing-impaired person to do so. She was first runner-up and won the talent award for a performance in dramatic sign language. Few realized she could not even hear the music she danced to.

I met this remarkable woman when she was just starting a professional speaking career. Her well-crafted, persuasive message was delivered with unforgettable style. She was obviously a rising star. Her silent life resounded with resilience.

As our friendship grew, I noticed how well supported Deirdre was by nurturing family and friends, and how she, in turn, shared her exuberant resilience with them. Her father told me that, as a child, Deirdre constantly inspired him because she never became bitter when others ridiculed her for her altered speech. With enormous perseverance, she learned to read lips and to speak with clarity and expression. (We often laughed together about the people who raised the decibel level when they spoke to her, somehow believing that the volume rather than clear enunciation would help her to read their lips!)

Deirdre captured the essence of a rock-solid self-image when she said, "Social acceptance is important, but not as important as self-acceptance. As a speaker, I cannot hear the audience's applause, but I've learned that the sweetest applause comes from within."

Her effervescent personality and zest for life attracted a young man named Steve Stanford. She told me that she fell in love with him the night he turned on the lights inside the car as they were driving so she could read his lips. She and Steve were soon married and starting a family.

But the illness that caused her deafness had also weakened her heart. She underwent two open-heart surgeries, the second to implant a pacemaker. She never complained, weathering the trial with dignity and grace, bouncing back even stronger and more determined than before.

Tragically, just six weeks after the birth of her second son, Deirdre Stanford died of a sudden heart attack. She was just thirty years old. Her family asked me to deliver her eulogy. It was a humbling experience to try to capture the essence of such an exceptional person, but I found comfort in knowing that her life, although short, had a completeness. She had been a mother, a wife, a friend, an educator, and an inspiration to many. She had used all her many resources to create the kind of life she wanted to have.

At the memorial service, her mother asked everyone to sing "Amazing Grace." Afterward, she thanked them, saying, "I'd always hoped that someday Deirdre could hear that song. Today I'm sure she did."

RESILIENCE BUILDER
Take a Personal Inventory

Each of us is positively bristling with unique and marvelous personal resources, yet some folks go around feeling bankrupt, incompetent, and ineffective. Stockpile your resilience now for when you'll need it by making a realistic inventory of your many resources.

1. Your Talents and Skills

Identify your best points. List your ten most positive attributes, attitudes, beliefs, and skills. (Be generous as well as honest!) If you have trouble getting started, go back to the questions under

"Resource #1." Remember to count it as a strength if you handle daily annoyances and irritations gracefully, or if you take common frustrations in stride.

2. Your Limitations

Identify your shortcomings. Write down ten things you usually struggle with or that you more or less have decided you can't change about yourself and must live with. Next, go back and *reevaluate* your assumptions! Then jot down how you compensate for these (perceived) faults. What resources and strategies do you use? How successful are they? What could you try in the future?

3. Role Models

Identify your sources of inspiration. Name the people who serve as the role models and mentors in the different aspects of your life—work, family, community, self, and any project or activity you feel passionate about. *(For more about how to choose a mentor, see Chapter 7.)*

Identify your sources of information. What people do you turn to for facts and advice about:

- finances
- work
- personal relationships
- social events and contacts
- personal style
- spiritual matters

Could you or should you expand this list?

4. Your Cheering Section

Identify your sources of support. When something good or bad happens, whom do you call and why? Who backs you up? Do you need to expand this list? If so, how will you do so?

Take a few minutes to look back over the people who've made a positive difference in your life. Besides your immediate family, who else has influenced you? A teacher? A coach, bus driver, janitor, camp counselor, neighbor or family friend, club leader, clergyman, maybe even the person behind the counter at your favorite store? What about employers? Your first boss? A coworker? Someone who influenced your career choice? Make a list. To share your resilience, write as many as possible a quick note, describing the differences they have made in your life.

5. Imagination

Recognize your script. Television buys scripts on the basis of a "treatment," a brief synopsis of the plot, made to sound as exciting and interesting as possible. Write a one-page treatment of your life.

6. Self-Acceptance

Identify your uniqueness. Imagine that you are standing in a huge crowd of people from every part of the world. You recognize all you have in common with your fellow humans, but in your heart, you know that you have some special qualities that few of them share. What are they?

7. A Healthy Body

If you don't already have a regular exercise program, start with *The Stamina Stroll.* You'll need a watch and a comfortable pair of shoes. Tomorrow, take a 15-minute walk on a level surface, seven minutes away from your door, seven minutes back. Each day, increase your time one minute until you're walking 30 minutes a day. Then slowly step up your speed, seeing how much extra distance you can cover. When you can walk a mile in 15 minutes, add small hand weights to your daily regime. Notice how much better you feel, how much extra bounce and resilience you've acquired.

8. Hope

Interconnectedness. Can you identify at least five things you do that connect you positively and interactively with your family, friends, neighbors, business colleagues, and community? If you can't, decide how to increase your interaction with others.

Hope objects. Choose some intensely personal objects or images that are especially meaningful to you—a photo of a loved one, a religious image, a memento of an important time—so that when you focus on them you are automatically flooded with a sense of well-being.

9. Faith and Prayer

Prayer is an unlimited resource. It is not only talking to God, but listening as well. Keep your ears open.

A Lifetime Resource

When baseball Hall of Famer Ty Cobb was nearing the end of his life, he was interviewed by a newspaper reporter. "Mr. Cobb," asked the young man, "if you were playing today, considering all the changes in Major League Baseball, what would your batting average be?"

It's important to remember that Ty Cobb was one of the greatest players of all time and had a lifetime batting average of .367. Cobb contemplated that question for a moment, looked at the reporter and said, "Well, if I were playing today, I'd probably bat about .290, maybe .300."

"I'm assuming, Mr. Cobb," the reporter said, "that's because more games are played each season than when you were playing, also the night games, the artificial turf and, unquestionably, because the pitchers today have a more effective arsenal of pitches. That's why you'd probably hit .290 or .300, right?"

Ty Cobb looked at him. "No," he said. "It's because I'm seventy years old." Self-image is everything!

6

Seize Responsibility

PAY YOURSELF FIRST

An impressive young man, Carlos Santori, was my driver to the airport from the Walt Disney World Swan Hotel in Orlando, Florida. As we drove along in the hotel van, he mentioned that we'd be taking side roads for a few miles instead of the Bee Line Expressway, but I wasn't to worry. The distance was the same, and we wouldn't lose any time because we wouldn't have to stop to pay the toll. Frankly, I wondered if he was pocketing the difference. "Do you know why I worked out this route?" he asked. You can bet I was curious.

"I did it to save the hotel money," Carlos told me. "Here at the Swan, we're always talking about empowerment and responsibility. We all understand that the little things make the big difference. Even though a dollar doesn't seem like much, I make a lot of these trips, and I feel I'm contributing to the bottom line."

Soon after, I called Nancy Lebrecht, director of human resources at the Swan Hotel, to gain some insight into their corporate culture. What was the Swan Hotel doing that encouraged this kind of personal initiative?

"We strive to make sure that everyone, from the top to the bottom, feels as if they have value," Nancy told me. "We want employees to be involved in designing their own work environment, one that encourages the growth and involvement of all employees. This way, they discover their own accountability."

Carlos Santori has grasped one of the key components of resilience: *responsibility.* While others are complaining "It's not my job," resilient people make the job their own and make a difference.

BOUNCE HIGHER TIP

Responsibility and resilience go together.
Winning and whining don't.

Responsibility: "Blame" or "Take Charge"?

Responsibility is both a *cause* and an *effect* of resilience. Think of it as "the ability to respond." The word has come to mean being dependable and not letting others down. However, the real damage you do to your resilience and self-image is when you let *yourself* down. Savvy financial managers say "pay yourself first." That's what you do when you keep your promises and commitments to others: You are paying yourself.

Real resilience isn't possible without a strong sense of responsibility: seeking out and seizing opportunities for commitment, as well as readily admitting errors so we can correct our course when things go wrong.

When people are feeling less than resilient, responsibility can be one of the hardest things in the world to deal with. If their self-image is weak, assets can start to seem like burdens, and possibilities like punishments. *Promises, assignments,* or *commitments* look less like "opportunities for growth" and more like "obligations that will drag me down."

What I have noticed about resilient individuals and organizations is that they see responsibility as positive. They believe they are active participants in their own fate, and they see themselves as victors, not victims. They know that no one else can give them self-respect, a positive self-image, or even resilience. And they see each responsible act as a powerful and valuable contribution to their own inner worth, not as a drain or a huge favor they're doing for someone else.

Resilient Thinking

- I am responsible for both my successes and my survival in the face of setbacks.
- My achievements and my failures are the direct result of my talents and how hard I try. Other factors may intervene, but ultimately it's up to me.
- My behavior is my own choice, not forced on me by events or the actions of others.

Less-resilient people tend to hand their power over to others. They doubt or deny that what they do and think makes any difference.

Nonresilient Thinking

- This always happens to me.
- It's all their fault.
- That's the way I am, so you might as well accept it.

Fragile egos also see responsibility as a blame game, so they try to protect themselves by avoiding it:

- If I don't take responsibility, no one will expect anything from me.
- If I'm not committed, I don't have to decide what I really want.
- If I don't commit to wanting something, no one can take it away from me and no one will notice that I didn't achieve it. That way, I can't fail.

Unfortunately, this solution is like quicksand. The harder these folks thrash around, trying to evade the trap of self-recrimination, the deeper they sink.

BOUNCE HIGHER TIP

If you find yourself caught in a negative loop and want to get out, start by claiming responsibility for just one thing.

Every time you honor a commitment or fulfill an obligation, you are building your resilience and making yourself stronger.

Who Owns Your Life?

Ken Pitman is the CEO of Euronet International, a large distributor of clothing and household goods based in Luxembourg. Since the fall of the Berlin Wall in 1990, he has been expanding his business into eastern Europe. Ken gave me a unique personal perspective on the connection between responsibility and resilience.

"After the wall came down," he told me, "people discovered that rights and freedoms came at a price. When we opened our operations in eastern Europe and began working with people who grew up under communism, we found a very different level of personal resilience than we were used to dealing with. With such limited freedoms, few of our new employees had developed any decision-making skills or accountability for their choices. We more or less had to offer a crash course in accountability. We had to convince them that they were responsible for their own future."

Ken found that some eastern Europeans had difficulty grasping a concept that most of us take for granted, that their actions could influence the outcome of their lives. This was a new belief system for them. Until then, they had been responsible only for conforming. If they turned up and went through the motions, that was enough. Now they were being held responsible for the results as well.

Such enormous change produced a backlash. "In the first flush of freedom, everyone was shouting, 'I want to be free!' " said Ken. "Then, six months later, when the economy was in turmoil and many were worse off economically than before, they were reminiscing about 'the good old days.' However, those who have been able to accept this new level of responsibility have forged ahead and been phenomenally successful."

"Whose Fault Is It?"

When you can claim responsibility for both the good and bad results of your actions and still stay optimistic, you're resilient! Attaining this level of resiliency isn't easy. People can't go from blaming others to taking personal responsibility overnight, just as they can't go from couch potato to champion athlete.

Responsibility starts when we understand the consequences of our actions—and inactions. Other people may make events easier or harder for us to get through, but we alone make the choices, and we alone are responsible for the outcome. The moment we accept this, our prospects for success and fulfillment rise. In an "it's-not-my-fault!" world, it pays to remember the sign President Harry S. Truman had on his desk: *The buck stops here.* We each need to post a similar sign in our psyche.

Before we can enjoy our successes, we have to acknowledge our stumbles. Resilient people claim full responsibility in all areas of their lives, *especially* when they've made a major mistake. Sure, such setbacks are never pleasant, but we rebuild our self-image and momentum faster when we concentrate on how to put things right. When we can do this, our progress is all the more rewarding. No one can take achievement away from us, because we *earned* it.

BOUNCE HIGHER TIP

When you want to encourage a greater sense of responsibility in others (and yourself), emphasize the anticipation of accomplishment, not the penalties for failure.

When threatened with success, low-resilience men and women figure out a way to sabotage themselves, so they can reconcile the mental mismatch between what's happening inside and outside themselves. Psychologists call this self-handicapping. As an athlete, I saw this often. If players were unprepared mentally and physically, they'd pull up lame halfway through the contest. This gave them a comfortable out. They could convince themselves that the game was lost because of an unavoidable injury, not through their lack of preparation.

The truly resilient often seize responsibility even when they could legitimately duck it. Aaron Feuerstein certainly wasn't responsible when his 130-year-old textile mill burned down. He's president of Malden Mills Industries in Lawrence, Massachusetts, the company that makes the popular Polartec and Polarfleece fabrics used in sports clothes. Three weeks before Christmas 1995, a fire injured thirty-three employees and put eighteen hundred people out of a job. In Lawrence, one of the poorest cities in the nation, this was a devastating blow both to the workers and to the entire community.

Feuerstein was seventy years old. He could have pocketed the insurance on his buildings and gone into a well-deserved retirement. Instead, within hours he had gathered his people together and made them a promise. The factory would be rebuilt. In the meantime, their salaries would continue for thirty days and their health insurance for ninety days. At the end of that thirty days, 65 percent of the employees were already back at work. Feuerstein continued full pay for those who weren't.

"Why am I doing it?" he responded to reporters amid the cheers of his workers. "I consider the employees . . . the most valuable asset that Malden Mills has. I don't consider them like some companies do, as an expense that can be cut. I know in the long run that what I'm doing today will come back tenfold and will make Malden Mills the best company in the industry."

On September 14, 1997, a dedication ceremony celebrated both the official opening of the new high-tech factory and Aaron Feuerstein's commitment to the people of Lawrence. All but seventy of his employees were back at work, with the remainder to return by the end of the year. Feuerstein's now-legendary loyalty to his employees had been reflected in increased customer loyalty, as well. In fact, Malden Mills had bounced back so far that they announced plans to hire an additional one hundred workers.

Your Power Cycle

Responsibility is sometimes called accountability, integrity, and even character. These words may seem similar, but each has distinctive characteristics. Together they form a three-legged support system for responsibility. If one of these supports is weak or missing—well, you know what happens when you cut one leg off a three-legged stool.

Character—Be responsible for your attitudes.
Accountability—Be responsible for your actions.
Integrity—Be responsible for your values.

Our attitudes and values are inexorably linked with our actions, each dependent on the other to create our sense of responsibility.

CHARACTER: YOUR ATTITUDES

"Character is the foundation of resilience," Dave Dougherty told me. He's president and CEO of Federated Group. "Reputation is what others think of you," Dave went on. "Character is what you do when no one is looking. We have to work hard all our lives so that our character and reputation match."

When you were a kid, you probably felt peer pressure to go along with the group, and some adult probably challenged you with, "Well, if everyone else was jumping off a cliff, would you have to do it too?" As adults, we can usually see the cliff and what lies below. Strong character means that our sense of self-worth is so strong that we can resist outside pressures and easy solutions.

The ultimate proof of character is realizing you're the only one on earth responsible for your own character. When you accept this responsibility, you earn respect from others as well as yourself.

Here's a good character check. Imagine that what you're doing is going to be featured on the front page of newspapers and on TV. How will you feel? Proud? Flattered? Great. But if you'd feel uncomfortable, even horrified, it's time to get your character in sync with the reputation you'd like to have. With rock-solid character, you have the resilience to face anything in life.

A Decision for Life

The Bettenhausen family was taking its annual skiing vacation in Colorado, savoring the exhilarating air, the glittering snow, the majestic mountains. All year they had looked forward to this trip. Then their twelve-year-old son Brian had a bad fall. He hit his head on a tree and was rushed to a hospital.

Doctors put him on a life-support system as his parents waited, praying that everything would be all right. Finally the word came. Tests showed there was no brain activity. His parents, Bob and Joanne, were faced with the agonizing decision about when to turn off the machines.

Before they signed the papers, they were told of the many people waiting for transplants. Here was a chance to make a decision for life in the midst of grief and death. They immediately agreed. As Bob told me, "Our son, who loved life and people so much, was able to give many others a new chance to live."

Their drive back home to Nebraska without Brian was the hardest journey Bob and Joanne had ever made. Despite their devastation, they clung to the knowledge that, because of Brian's gift, lives would be saved and sightless eyes would see.

"We felt good about the donor decision," Bob told me, "and we knew our son would have wanted it that way. However, not everyone in our immediate family felt as we did, so for many years we never mentioned the subject." Then one winter morning nine years later, just after Thanksgiving, something happened that caused Bob and Joanne to break their silence.

They were awakened by a phone call from a woman who said, "I'm trying to reach the parents of Brian Bettenhausen." When she learned she had the right number, she told them her name was Darlene Wilson. She lived near Denver, and ever since the transplant surgery, she had wanted to locate them. "My son Mark is alive today," she told them, "because he received one of your son's kidneys."

Mark's kidneys had been damaged by complications of a strep infection when he was four years old. His parents were told that he would be able to lead a fairly normal life, but sooner or later his kidneys would fail. He was twenty years old when this happened.

Transplant programs are reluctant to disclose the identities of organ donors and recipients because of potential emotional complications. The Wilsons were told only that Mark's donor was a twelve-year-old boy who had died in a skiing accident. However, it didn't take them long to figure out Brian's identity. The front page of the *Denver Post* told about Brian Bettenhausen of Lincoln, Nebraska, who had died in a skiing accident at Keystone Ski Resort. Darlene Wilson was told that the donor family had left the state, and that she was not to try to contact them. But she never stopped being grateful to the Bettenhausens.

Nine years later, she was driving from Denver to Chicago and stopped at a motel in Lincoln, Nebraska. The next morning, on a hunch, she looked up "Bettenhausen" in the local phone book. She decided to call one of the several families listed. "We know it wasn't an accident that she got us on the first try," says Bob.

The Bettenhausens learned that Mark Wilson had married and was finishing a degree in business. Mark had also participated in the Transplant Olympics and won two gold medals. Mark had always loved sports, but until his surgery he'd been physically limited by his kidney condition. "Brian was also an athlete and avid sports fan," Bob told me, "so he'd really have loved that."

"The thing that touched our hearts most," Bob said, "was learning that Mark wanted to do something in Brian's memory." Mark had already put as much of Brian's last name as he could on his license plate, which reads, BETTEN. Most people who ask about it think it refers to gambling. Certainly, an organ transplant *is* a gamble, and the plate gives Mark a chance to tell people about the twelve-year-old who gave him a new chance at life.

"To learn all this almost nine years after our son's accident, especially since we'd been told we would never know who the recipients were, was absolutely the neatest Christmas gift we've ever received. We profoundly hope others will never have to go through the terrible heartbreak we experienced, but we encourage everyone facing this decision to choose the organ-donor program. Through it, Brian was able to give the gift of life to more than eighteen people."

"What fueled your resilience?" I asked Bob.

He thought carefully. "What I tell people," he said, "is to find ways to help others. It's what keeps you going, and it's the only way to give meaning to what you've lost. Our family has always believed that you'll be judged by what you give, not what you take."

ACCOUNTABILITY: YOUR ACTIONS

Accountability is a decision: You decide that your effort or lack of effort is a major factor in determining your success or lack of success. It's easy to *say* you believe this, but not always easy to do. Both accountability and resilience are impossible until you recognize the control you have over your destiny.

In some environments, "accountability" means punishment and liability. Fixing blame becomes more important than fixing problems. It's doubly hard to nurture your own sense of accountability when you're likely to get a blast instead of a boost every time you stick your neck out.

In this less-than-perfect world, resilient people grit their teeth and accept that not everything they do will be appreciated or rewarded. The decision is up to them: either they can focus on protecting their backsides from attack, or they can decide to be responsible for their own sense of responsibility. When they accept accountability and are less than successful, they can ask themselves:

- What extra steps could I have taken?
- What should I have avoided?
- What can I do differently now and in the future?

When it's a choice between letting things ride or choosing accountability, resilient people choose accountability every time. You can count on them to do what they say they will, because they have made a habit of dependability. Every time you honor your commitments, you build your self-confidence. The person ultimately responsible for your happiness, well-being, and resilience is *you*.

Choosing to Connect with Others

I learned early in my life that it was my responsibility to help others respond to me positively. This is true for all of us. I cannot control other people's reactions, but I *can* take responsibility for connecting with them warmly and positively. Whenever I meet someone for the first time, I stand up straight, speak in a friendly, confident voice, stretch out my right hand for a handshake, and smile.

Two fascinating things can happen when I do this. One is that almost everyone responds in kind. The other is that a few people reply in a loud voice, as if they fear I am deaf. (Once, I watched skycaps bring a smiling woman in a wheelchair off the plane. A group of waiting friends laughed and cheered as she appeared. One of her legs was in a cast, one arm was in a cast, and around her neck was a sign: I'm Not Deaf! I Just Broke My Arm and Leg Skiing.)

How do you meet and greet people? When you run into strangers and acquaintances, do your words and gestures (or lack of them) indicate indifference or discomfort? Or can you convey your pleasure at the encounter so they get the subliminal message, "Meeting you has made my day"?

All of us are responsible for how we speak and how we listen to strangers and friends, to our family and our coworkers. Non-resilient people can see this as a burden, but the resilient find it liberating and empowering. It puts you in charge of your life.

Choosing to Lead

How do you say *accountability* in Polish? How do you even explain the concept to fledgling businesses in a country that has had nothing resembling a free economy since before World War I?

This was the challenge that Sheila Murray Bethel and Bill Bethel took on in December 1990, shortly after the fall of the Berlin Wall and the end of communism in Europe. Earlier that year, while Sheila was on the interview circuit promoting her book on leadership, one of the ideas that brought the most comments was her proposal for a Leadership Corps, similar to the Peace Corps. She advocated the creation of a program to send America's top business and community leaders all over the world to share their knowledge about how to lead in a free economy.

Then, one day in August 1990, George Bush mentioned in a speech that he'd like to form a volunteer Leadership Corps. Instantly, Sheila was on the phone to the White House, trying to find out who would be organizing it and what she could do to help. After several attempts, she finally reached a White House consultant who had just been assigned to do preliminary work on the idea. Through him, Sheila and Bill connected with the American representative of the Polish Solidarity movement.

Sheila's White House contact reported that there were no appropriations for the project, but that something might be organized in about eighteen months. "I didn't feel that Poland *had* eighteen months," Sheila told me. "They were in a tremendous state of flux and on the eve of their first democratic elections."

There are fascinating psychological studies showing that the more people who observe someone in distress or a disaster in the making, the less likely it is that any one person will take action. Each reasons that because others see the same calamity and are doing nothing, nothing can be done. But this negative group dynamic is broken when one person steps forward. It can take enormous personal courage to step out of the crowd and take responsibility.

This is one reason why I admire Sheila and Bill so much. They decided to be the ones to step forward. ("If not me, who?") After much soul-searching, they put their lives on hold, got out their own checkbooks, and set about organizing a speaking tour of Poland.

Four months after Bush's speech, Bill and Sheila arrived in Warsaw on a very cold December day. Then for fourteen days, eighteen hours a day, they stood in factories, stores, meeting halls, and private homes throughout southern Poland, explaining to thousands of eager listeners the fundamentals of a free-enterprise economy that we all take for granted: writing a strategic business plan, marketing, the customer-service ethic, the sales process, team building, and accountability.

"It was the most intense experience of my life," Sheila says.

"We explained how businesses work in the world's free economy, but stressed that they are going to have to find their own solutions."

At one factory they met a man who wanted to start a second business because he and his partner had gone as far as they could locally. Their three hot-sausage carts were as many as their small town could support. He hoped the Bethels could recommend another enterprise.

Bill and Sheila stared at him. "Why don't you have pushcarts in other towns and start a chain?" they asked. "You could end up with hundreds of them from here to Warsaw."

An enormous, blinding light went on. Such a possibility had simply never occurred to him. Under communism, you didn't travel to the next town to visit your mother, much less to sell something, without special dispensation from the police department.

Any individual or nation seeking role models for resilient accountability need look no farther than Bill and Sheila. Bill told me how the people they met were constantly taking hold of their hands and looking into their eyes. "There was one phrase they repeated over and over," Sheila added, "until finally we didn't need a translator to understand it." Here Sheila stopped and tears came to her eyes. "They said, 'God has sent you to us. Please don't forget us.' "

INTEGRITY: YOUR VALUES

Integrity is character in action. Nonresilient people let society establish standards, then try to live up to them. Resilient people look at society's code of ethics as a Minimum Daily Requirement—and then set higher goals for themselves. The payoff in self-respect is enormous.

All of us have faced moral dilemmas. How we confront them (or fail to confront them) defines our integrity, standards, and values. *Integral* means an essential part of the whole, and *integrity* means that you are whole, that your inner values and outer behavior match. When you believe one thing and do another, you're in deep trouble.

Some common ways that people seduce themselves into avoiding responsibility are:

- Nobody will ever know. (But *you* know!)
- It's not important. (Isn't it?)
- I have a right to do that. (But is it the right thing to do?)
- Everyone else is doing it. (Does that mean you must do it?)

Excuses like these disempower and sabotage us. When what we do clashes with our belief system, we attack our own self-respect and resilience. It's something like those signs in parking lots that warn you about severe tire damage if you go the wrong way. Every time your actions conflict with your values and you go the "wrong way," you're inflicting severe damage on yourself.

BOUNCE HIGHER TIP

Every time you keep a promise or fulfill a commitment, recognize that you are rewarding yourself.

Sometimes people make promises under pressure just to get someone off their back. It's easier than saying "No" or "I don't want to." Be sure you commit yourself only to promises that you want to keep and can keep. If you find it hard to follow through, seek out others for guidance and counsel. Identify the people whose integrity you admire, then emulate them. Start stockpiling reserves of integrity and self-respect.

Taking the High Road

You might not know Billy Demby's name, but you've probably seen his commercial. He was featured in a DuPont TV ad that showed him playing basketball while wearing two artificial legs.

During the Vietnam War, Billy lost both his legs below the knee when his jeep ran over a land mine. It was a miracle that he survived at all. When he left the United States for Vietnam, he was an outstanding athlete, one of the best high school basketball players in the country. When he returned, he couldn't walk.

Billy pioneered technology for amputees and worked with DuPont to develop new materials and products that benefit people throughout the world. I asked him how he did it. "First I had to learn to walk," he told me. "Then I had to *reinvent my life.*"

Think about that: *"Reinvent your life."* Billy drew on his past achievements, he evaluated his resources, and he took responsibility for his life. As part of taking that responsibility, he reached a point where he could adjust his focus from his own needs to those of others. That's a powerful demonstration of resilience, and an enormously useful technique when things go wrong.

I was struck by Billy's integrity, even in the small details of life. In the DuPont commercial, we see him approaching a basketball court. A group of young men watches as he removes his warm-up pants, revealing his two prostheses. Then you see Billy walk out onto the court. Someone throws him a ball, and Billy begins the game. He competes as an equal, and the other players are amazed at his agility and winning spirit.

This memorable commercial won numerous awards, but Billy told me that it almost didn't get made. The producer had asked him, "How high can you jump?" Billy jumped as high as he could—only a few inches. "Don't worry, Billy," the producer told him. "We can make you look like Superman by how we edit the tape."

Billy was faced with a difficult choice. He could go along with some innocent "movie magic" and look like Michael Jordan, soaring through the air. This would make the commercial much more dramatic. After all, few people believe that raisins really dance or that rabbits leap out of cereal boxes.

But then Billy began to think about his responsibility to others. Would this give able-bodied people an unrealistic idea of what life as an amputee was like? How would other amputees react? Billy decided that he couldn't do the commercial unless it was shot realistically. Billy's personal sense of responsibility and integrity was persuasive. The producer respected his decision and agreed. Because Billy had taken the high road, an award-winning commercial was made with total integrity.

When It's Really Not Your Fault

What is up to you and what isn't? As I was considering the life experiences of people I know who have rebounded after hard times, I noticed that all these people had one ability in common: They were able to separate what they *were* responsible for from what they *weren't*. When we try to assume responsibility for situations beyond our control, we actually erode our resilience.

> **BOUNCE HIGHER TIP**
>
> *If you're responsible: do it, fix it, resolve it.*
> *But don't waste a moment blaming yourself*
> *for what you can't control.*

After I spoke about responsibility at a recent conference, a young couple approached me and asked if they could share a personal story.

A year and a half before, they had given birth to a healthy boy. He was the delight of their lives, and they were overwhelmed with joy. During the next few months, they were so concerned they might not hear him cry at night that they kept him between them in their bed. They knew they were being overcautious, and the father finally decided that his son should sleep in a bassinet in the corner of their room. The mother objected, but he insisted. Tragically and incredibly, the first night that the child spent in the bassinet, he died of Sudden Infant Death Syndrome (SIDS).

After the funeral, the devastated young couple locked themselves in their house for several days. Even though their doctor had confirmed that it was just a terrible coincidence, this young man decided that he was responsible for the baby's death because he had insisted on the bassinet. His wife was torn with grief and anger.

Still searching for answers, they joined a nearby SIDS support group. There they began to accept that the baby's death was beyond their control. They hadn't caused it, nor could they have prevented it. Gradually, they let go of their guilt and self-blame.

What struck me as I was talking to them was how much focus they had regained. Professionally, they had been chosen as delegates to attend this conference; personally, they had found the courage to have another child.

Their experiences helped me clarify my own thinking about responsibility. This young couple told me that they had to separate what they were ultimately responsible for from what was beyond their control. Only then could they rebuild their lives, their resilience, and their personal happiness.

"Who, Me?"

Imagine an elegant conference setting. Then picture two hundred very dignified, very professional businesspeople who have been concentrating hard all day.

It started innocently enough. I was doing a presentation at the beautiful Hotel Del Coronado in San Diego when the afternoon break was announced. Most of the conference-goers streamed out into the hall to stretch and talk.

A few moments later, a waiter came through the service doors about twenty yards down the hall, pushing a big cart. On it were giant trays of the largest, most delicious-looking chocolate-chip cookies I've ever seen. They were the size of Frisbees, and the smell, even from where we stood, was sensational. In the center of this mountain of delectability were crystal pitchers of milk, resting in silver basins of crushed ice.

The waiter disappeared through the service doors. There was dead silence. Two hundred people stood goggle-eyed and drooling at this unexpected vision. Perhaps the waiter had left their refreshments next to the wrong door. No one knew quite what to do.

Then, very slowly, one man sauntered down the hall to the cart. He looked this way. He looked that way. Then he selected a cookie and took a bite. Next he poured himself a big glass of ice-cold milk and took a sip. He smiled.

A second person followed him, then a third. You could tell by the way they walked that they weren't entirely sure they were doing the right thing, but the aroma of those cookies was irresistible. In a few minutes, everyone was gathered around the cart.

Suddenly the door next to the cart opened, revealing another room full of people. A startled voice shrieked, "Hey! Those cookies are for *our* meeting!"

Like a bunch of little kids who'd been caught doing something naughty, these very dignified executives scampered in every direction. They literally ran.

The woman in charge of the other conference was understandably irate. Such a succulent snack had taken quite a bit of planning, and now her people were left with only crumbs and empty glasses. She stormed over to the man in charge of our conference with blood in her eyes and murder in her heart. He backed away from her angry onslaught, apologizing profusely but protesting that he really knew nothing about what had happened.

From the safety of my spot just inside the meeting-room doorway, I watched him try to defuse her tirade as he vigorously denied responsibility. He might have been a bit more convincing if he hadn't had a noticeable milk mustache and cookie crumbs all down his shirt.

PROFILE

In-N-Out Burger

There are burgers. And then there are In-N-Out burgers. They're made from never-frozen beef, topped with sliced-on-the-spot tomatoes, lettuce, and onions, and served on chemical-free, slow-baked buns with french fries that are peeled and sliced minutes before you bite into them, then washed down with one of their incredible malted milks, made the old-fashioned way, right in front of your eyes, with real ice cream. In other words, they're awesome!

But the In-N-Out story is about more than food. It's the saga of several highly responsible and resilient people who followed an ideal, despite stunning setbacks. In 1948, the founders of In-N-Out Burger, Harry and Esther Snyder, demonstrated their integrity and responsibility by deciding to offer the best rather than the cheapest. To keep costs reasonable, they dispensed with the traditional carhops who took orders and delivered food to parked cars, often in exotic costumes and on roller skates. Instead, customers were sped on their way with a brand-new device, a two-way speaker box to take orders. California's first drive-through fast-food stand was born. The Snyders bet on Californians' twin addictions to automobiles and hamburgers, and they won big.

In-N-Out had gone from a single hamburger stand in Baldwin Park to a chain of eighteen locations when Harry Snyder died in 1976. One son, Rich, became president at age twenty-four, while the other son, Guy, became vice president, concentrating on new quality-control technology. Esther Snyder continued as secretary and treasurer.

The Snyders felt accountable to their customers, so the first thing Rich and Guy changed was . . . absolutely nothing. No tinkering with the menu or the recipes or company policy. (For example, In-N-Out still pays more than the industry wage standard because "we want the best sixteen- and seventeen-year-olds out there.")

I met the Snyders in 1991, and was struck by their loyalty to their employees and their employees' obvious loyalty to them.

Rich, Guy, and Esther had established a healthy culture with the Power Cycle of Responsibility as its basis. Every action and company policy demonstrated personal character, public integrity, and a deep sense of accountability to employees and customers alike.

Then, in December 1993, tragedy struck.

Just before Christmas, Rich was returning from a business trip. He, the company's executive vice president of administration, and another employee had flown to northern California to attend the opening of a new store. They followed company policy of taking separate planes, but on the return trip everyone was tired. For the final leg, they decided to fly together. Just a short hop together, just this once, in a small private plane, would bring all the weary travelers home. The plane never made it; there were no survivors.

Such a blow would cripple or destroy some companies, but the In-N-Out people demonstrated remarkable resilience. "Because we had a clear vision for the future, we all felt a responsibility to fulfill it," said Rich's brother, Guy. "It was impossible not to go on."

Matriarch Esther Snyder, though grief-stricken herself, immediately set about consoling everyone. "Her incredible strength amazed us all," Guy told me. "The organization had lost its CEO, but she had lost a son." Esther spoke at the funeral, and, within a week, she and Guy met with the store managers to go over their concerns. She also videotaped a message for all the hourly employees, assuring them that nothing was going to change.

Guy Snyder quickly took over as chief executive officer and chairman of the board, and he appointed Esther as president because he wanted her to maintain a strong presence in the company. Today, Esther has been in the business more than fifty years, and she still goes to the office every day.

"Where did you find the resilience to face such a loss?" I asked her. Esther told me that she drew strength from the past, remembering how she had survived the loss of her husband seventeen years earlier. These memories brought her comfort and peace. Guy added, "Our values of faith, responsibility, and commitment were the underlying fabric that held us together."

RESILIENCE BUILDER
Seizing Responsibility
1. Use Take-Charge Language

Here are seven responsibility-avoiding statements that don't belong in a resilient vocabulary:

- "That's not my job."
- "I'll try to get around to it."
- "I think someone else is taking care of that."
- "No one ever asked me."
- "No one ever told me."
- "Why pick on me?"
- "Who cares, anyway?"

Have you used any of them recently? If so, rewrite the scene, casting yourself in a positive, active, responsible role.

2. Write Your Own Recommendation

Imagine that you're someone else, and you've been asked to write a letter of recommendation for *you*. Complete the following statements:

- My level of confidence in this person is:
- A recent example of this person's integrity is:
- I can always depend on this person for:
- However, some situations where this person might be less than responsible are:
- This is because:
- Overall, his/her reputation is:

What have you learned about yourself? Would you want to hire this person? Have him or her for a friend? Trust him or her with your secrets? With your savings? With your life? If so, congratulations! If not, what will you change and how?

3. Try This Energizer

Think about something difficult that you "should" take responsibility for, perhaps something that you should solve or resolve. Notice how your mind suddenly closes up, your eyelids droop, and your whole body feels weighted down. Now, imagine that you've just gotten a complicated new video game (or car engine or knitting pattern—anything that you usually find exciting). Notice how your brain engine suddenly turns over and your blood starts pumping. Resilient folks consciously trick and cajole themselves into a video-game intensity for disagreeable tasks, making a "game" out of a grind.

A Tank Full of Air

One morning I was hurrying to catch a plane. I glanced down at my gas gauge, saw it was near empty, and turned into the next gas station. There I threw my car into park, raced to the payment booth, thrust a twenty-dollar bill into the attendant's hand, and shouted, "Fill 'er up!" Back at my car, I leaped into the driver's seat and roared out of the gas station onto Highway 680, heading toward the San Francisco Airport. Five miles later, I noticed that my gas gauge was on empty.

What could have happened? Immediately, I began explaining the problem to myself. "That's how those gas stations keep their profit margins up—they put air in their pumps instead of gas.— No, that couldn't have been it. I know! I ran over something sharp that poked a hole in my gas tank so all the gas drained out on the highway.—No . . . I know what happened. Someone pulled up next to me at fifty-five miles per hour, stuck a hose in my tank, and siphoned the gas into their tank."

Then I remembered. I'd run in, paid the attendant, jumped in my car, and driven away without pumping any gas. I began to laugh so hard that I had to pull over.

Ultimately, we're all responsible for keeping our own gas tanks filled. (And, yes, I still managed to catch my plane.)

PART THREE

"Where Are You Going?"

YOUR MOTIVATIONS

My uncle, Orin Welsh, worked on the assembly line at Timken Steel in Canton, Ohio, for thirty-three years. I'll never forget the first time I got to watch him on the job.

Climbing to a scaffold high above the floor, I looked down on the cauldrons of boiling metal as they were tipped into molds. With the choking heat, the din, and occasional explosions of fiery sparks, it looked like a scene from Dante's *Inferno* or a *Batman* comic book.

Men were everywhere, dark shapes outlined against the glare as they poured and manipulated the white-hot steel. Then I spotted my uncle. He was walking along the edge of a trough, and he carried a huge pair of tongs. As six-foot rods of glowing steel rolled past him, my uncle grabbed them with his tongs and kept them on track. He wore no protective clothing, only overalls and heavy work boots. One small miscalculation or lapse in concentration and he'd have been terribly injured or worse.

Boy, was I impressed. Uncle Orin immediately became a larger-than-life figure to me, like the mythical steel-driving man, John Henry. I asked him, "Are you ever afraid you'll be hurt?" And when Uncle Orin told me his secret, he loomed even larger.

"Roger," he said. "You just don't look where you don't want to go."

Isn't that true for all resilient people? Concentrate on the path ahead, not on possible setbacks, disappointments, or hardships. *Don't look where you don't want to go!*

Your Third Set of Keys

The next three chapters are about how your *motivation* builds your personal resilience.

7. Harness the Power of Purpose. Having clear goals is the hallmark of resilience.

8. Develop Your Inborn Leadership. Resilience is charismatic.

9. Embrace Challenges. Preparation is the key to bouncing higher.

We've explored *attitudes* in the three keys to personal resilience described in Part I and *self-image* in the three keys of Part II. Now it's time to go to work on the future. What *motivates* you, excites you, puts the gas in your tank?

No amount of effort will override a negative attitude, but we can accomplish great things once our attitudes, self-image, and sense of purpose are in alignment. When you can answer the third question, "Where am I going?" you set yourself in motion.

Why does this book talk about attitudes first, self-image second, and motivations last? Because nonresilient people need to change their attitudes and fortify their self-image before they can motivate themselves.

Resilient people are at their most flexible when their path is blocked, because potential distractions and diversions only stimulate them and increase their motivation. They never stop concentrating on where they want to end up.

Be patient as you take these final steps to motivation that will lock in your resilience. There is no magic formula or pill you can take to speed up the project or make it effortless. Any worthwhile goal requires discipline, exertion, and strategy. Expect to succeed, but remember that "wanting it all *now*" is your enemy. You can't arrive without making the journey.

7

Harness the Power of Purpose

CREATE AN ACTION PLAN

My passion for football taught me the power of purpose. I started with backyard games after school and progressed to a place on the eighth-grade football team. As a defensive end, my assignment was to tackle the other team's players, but I was also permitted to recover fumbles and intercept passes. My goal, naturally, was to score a touchdown.

One day everything went right. A member of the other team was tackled and hit the ground hard. The football he was carrying went flying straight up in the air. I tilted my head back and watched that ball go up, up, in what seemed like slow motion. Then it came down and landed right in my arms.

I turned and raced down the field, hugging that ball to my chest. My teammates were running along beside me, trying to clear the way, and the crowd was cheering so loudly that the roar echoed in my helmet.

Suddenly I lurched. I'd been grabbed from behind in a "shoe-string tackle" on the ten-yard line. The guy was hanging on to my leg, and he wasn't about to let go. The goal was just ahead. I dragged him a few yards down the field as I struggled to jerk my leg free.

Instead, it came off in his hands.

I was still standing, so I kept going, hopping those last few yards. The referee threw his arms in the air. Touchdown! I was hopping up and down to keep my balance, and the crowd was hopping up and down cheering, and my coach was hopping up and down yelling and whooping. I'd made my touchdown. But almost as good as the six points I'd scored was the baffled look on the face of the kid who was still standing there, holding my artificial leg.

In my case, the end zone was clearly defined, but few things in life are that simple. Our lives are full of conflicting demands, choices, and distractions. Yet, it's impossible to stay resilient without having clear objectives and practical strategies for reaching them. Resilient people are constantly establishing goals because they are eager to stretch themselves beyond their current level of achievement.

You start by choosing and achieving an objective. First just one small attainment, and then another and another, each making the resilient spirit stronger. Great achievements are made up of small achievements. Motivational muscles are built like physical ones, slowly but surely. I like to break goal-seeking into a five-part process, the "5 E's."

1. **Expectations**—Turn your dreams into concrete goals.
2. **Execution**—Plan your journey.
3. **Expertise**—Acquire needed skills and get outside help.
4. **Endurance**—Maintain your motivation and energy.
5. **Evaluation**—Stay on track, making midcourse corrections.

1. EXPECTATIONS

All of us have vast resources of untapped potential within us, but none of us can access this potential until we *expect* to succeed. The mistake many people make is setting their expectations too low. Then they fail to mobilize all their talents and resources—which, in turn, lowers their self-regard and level of achievement. The true tragedy of an unresilient life is having low expectations—and then fulfilling them. Resilient people access their full potential by setting clear goals that will expand their expectations.

All great goals start out as vague dreams, a longing for something that seems beyond our reach. (Herman Lay, founder of Frito-Lay, the largest snack-food company on earth, says, "Don't tell me something is impossible. I founded this company with a potato.") The word *dream* implies something insubstantial and unachievable, but every achievement is built on one foundation of a dream. Some of us are content just to dream. (How many people drive down the freeway fantasizing about sailing their own boat around the world or climbing Mount Everest?) Resilient people also love to daydream, but then they decide which of their dreams deserve to become realities. In effect, they "dream in living color," creating a clear image of what they want to achieve.

We all love to hear about people who were told they couldn't do something and then did it anyway with great success. Fran Drescher was told her acting career would be limited unless she lost her New York accent. Instead, she turned her adenoidal "New Yawk"ese into an asset, producing her own hit sitcom, *The Nanny*. Pundits told Ted Turner that an all-news television channel was bound to fail, that TV news had become a loss leader, and that many stations were severely curtailing their news gathering. Turner started CNN anyway, and it's now a worldwide network. Everyone assured Steve Largent that he was too slow to play professional football. Yet he became the most prolific pass receiver in history.

What we often forget is that these winners paid their dues

because they expected to succeed. They established expectations and then took ownership of them. Fran Drescher played hundreds of small-time club dates and appeared in dozens of minor film and TV roles, honing her craft while deciding that what she did best was portray her own roots. Ted Turner had already demonstrated his business and risk-taking savvy as owner of the Atlanta Braves and the Atlanta Hawks. Steve Largent understood his own strengths and skills, and developed them to perfection. His precision accuracy in running pass patterns and his ability to exploit an opposing defensive back's weaknesses put him in the Pro Football Hall of Fame.

All three of these people knew their goals were within their grasps. They had assessed their resources and found innovative ways to use them, then worked hard to get where they wanted to be. So never stop dreaming. Just be willing to back up your dream with solid assets.

Finding What Excites You

Enthusiasm is the high-octane fuel that powers the goal-seeking process and keeps it going. When you're energized by your dreams and your goals, great things start to happen. If you lack this excitement, you're going to stall out before you even start.

Excitement is one of the simplest but surest motivators. It encourages full concentration and total engagement. Whenever we're enthusiastic, we become alert, inspired, and highly resilient. Dedicated goal seekers add the childlike zest of enthusiasm to their commitment. They have learned to see everyday chores as part of a larger, more exciting vision.

Daily goal: Keep my checkbook balanced.
Achievement goal: Feel the power of controlling my finances.

Daily goal: Remember to pack a healthful lunch when fast food is going to be the only other option.

Achievement goal: Feel good about my body and what I put in it!

In the larger context of achievement goals, no everyday task is ever trivial.

Sometimes people tell me they are really discouraged. "I set goals, but I never get anywhere," they say, or "I can't accomplish anything, no matter how hard I try." I ask them to start by telling me what daily goals they have achieved in the past week. Their answers can range from "getting up on time" to "clearing my in-box." As they recognize that they've actually set and accomplished these goals, I can literally see their confidence (and resilience) begin to build. Their excitement level rises and they are energized to take on more-demanding achievement goals.

Line Up Your Values

Someone once said that success is finding something in your life that you love to do, then finding someone to pay you to do it. In fact, "success" can mean very different things to different people. Just be sure that you're the one who writes your own definition. Ask yourself:

- What do I want to achieve in life?
- What makes me feel more alive?

When you can answer these two questions truthfully, and your answers match and support each other, you have defined success for yourself.

Professional fulfillment is just one aspect of success. As I said in Chapter 4, personal wealth comes in many forms—physical, mental, spiritual, and social. The truly resilient develop passionate goals in each of these areas.

Conduct a Reality Check

Aiming high is admirable, but setting goals so lofty that they are unattainable can sabotage your resilience. Build in provisions for meeting challenges and experiencing setbacks. Then you won't be deterred by struggle, discouragement, or even what seems like failure.

Joe Fields, CEO of Pentland Sports Group, told me that he starts with two questions when he is setting expectations for himself and his organization.

- Is this goal within reason? (Is it *practical?*)

The goal of becoming a pilot may be impractical if you suffer from severe air sickness. However, the goal of working in the aeronautics industry and being around planes on a daily basis is completely realistic.

- Is this goal within reach? (Is it *possible?*)

The goal of being a pro football player would be impossible for a ninety-eight-pounder, but the goal of experiencing triumph and exhilaration through sports is entirely possible.

When you can answer yes to both these questions you're ready to tackle anything you choose.

2. EXECUTION

Every dream castle needs a solid foundation, and every vision needs a practical action strategy. Once you've chosen your destination, it's time to design your travel itinerary. The difference between those who gain mastery and those who simply dream is their commitment to action. To achieve maximum resilience, you need to create an Action Plan that incorporates both your visions and your personal values, supported by both *outcome* goals and *performance* goals.

Making Your Action Plan

Some people put more energy into planning a weekend getaway or what to wear to a job interview than into designing a strategy for reaching their life's ambitions. Your life is worth a formal Action Plan. Like a good travel agent, you can make getting there as exciting and rewarding as being there.

A strong, workable Action Plan involves more than just deciding on a goal. It requires built-in structure and supports.

Set Clear, Measurable Outcome and Performance Goals. Write them down, avoiding vague or hard-to-define concepts and time frames. ("I will have my own business in two years. To achieve this, I will earn my license and arrange financing.")

Establish Short-term Objectives. Write down the daily, weekly, and/or monthly "stepping-stones" that will move you toward your long-term goals. ("I will do five hours of classes a week so I can earn my preliminary certification by March and full certification by next January. I will bank $50 a week toward the $5,000 start-up costs.")

Choose Visual Aids. Pick an image that will help you stay on track. It can be a stimulating mental picture or something you carry or wear to remind you of your goal. There's lots of room for creativity and fun here. ("I'll put a mock-up of my business logo on my refrigerator.")

Write a Realistic Timetable. Be practical and hardheaded about how long it's going to take you. Then keep a mental log of how you're spending your time. Are you consistently working toward your target? Or do you let other things distract you? If so, either refocus your energy or reconsider your goals. ("Shall I go to Hawaii or keep saving a few more months to reach my goal?")

Plan Rewards for Reaching Interim Goals. Give yourself an early reward for getting started, then motivate yourself with anticipation of a treat when you've achieved a particular objective. ("Every time I complete an assignment for class, I'll take a break and read a chapter in my mystery novel.")

Decide How You'll Know When You've Arrived. This is why vague goals like "success" or "happiness" don't work. Write a specific finish line into your plan. What will have happened? What will be different? What will you do next? ("I'll send out announcements to current clients when I get my certification. And I'll throw a great party for my friends. Then my five-year business plan goes into effect.")

Outcome and Performance Goals

Every effort involves both a process and a product. The effort needed to achieve goals follows this pattern. Individuals and organizations maintain resilience by having two different kinds of goals: **outcome goals** and **performance goals**.

Outcome goals tend to be defined as win/lose or success/failure. You reach them or you don't.

Performance goals acknowledge and reward quality, initiative, creativity, and innovation.

Remember that if you enter a race and come in dead last, you're still a winner. You've had the experience and gained much by the performance. The only loser is the one who never entered the race.

Resilient goal-seekers are willing to write risk taking and mistakes into their Action Plans. This trial-and-error approach is critical to the goal-achieving process. There is only one person you should be competing with: yourself. If you are always measuring yourself against someone else, your preoccupation with them throws you off track.

Make your performance goals as specific and measurable as outcome goals. For example, decide on a specific number of daily sales calls to be completed or a certain percentage of first serves to be made during a tennis match. The ongoing energy boosts you get from achieving these performance goals propel you toward your outcome goal. (Use this same strategy when you're helping others set group goals.)

Start by defining your performance and progress goals clearly. Write them down. What immediate steps do you need to take? What future steps? Divide your ultimate objectives into smaller segments—into *sub*goals—so you can judge your progress and keep on schedule. Write down these subgoals too. If your list gets too long, separate it even further into manageable, measurable units. Richard Weylman, a leading marketing expert and author of *Opening Closed Doors*, once told me that, when he embarked on a year-long project, he established 365 subgoals to gauge his progress!

I believe that we can achieve almost anything if we break the process down into enough pieces. If you make your increments too big, it's easy to feel overwhelmed by the distance between where you are and where you'd like to be. Everyone knows the saying, A journey of a thousand miles begins with a single step, yet how many of us truly act on this belief?

Take, for example, our national pastime of trying to lose weight. (As a traveling speaker, with all the banquet food I eat, the only thing I can count on is thin lips.) Judging by the number of diet-food ads, the number of diet foods sold, and the endless diet plans featured in magazines and newspapers, we should be the thinnest nation on earth. But we aren't, and I can suggest a possible reason. Most weight-loss programs promise dramatic results in a short time, and most people who try the special foods and regimens fail to reach their goals. They expect too much too soon, and then when they fail to get it, they give up.

Keep yourself (and others) motivated by continually recognizing and celebrating effort and progress as well as results.

Measurable, clearly defined outcome goals give us targets, but without performance goals, we can feel that all our time and effort was wasted if we don't reach our outcome goals. Let's say you decide that you want to own your own business, so you learn everything you can about financing, management, marketing, advertising, and labor relations. If, despite all your efforts, you fail to achieve your outcome goal, you have still acquired invaluable knowledge and skills that you can use in many ways. The *outcome* evaluation is that you failed to achieve your goal. The *performance* evaluation is that you have had many successes.

BOUNCE HIGHER TIP

*Use ambitious outcome goals
to achieve greatness.
Use daily performance goals
to achieve the true riches of life.*

Kentucky Fried Performance Goals

What's the best-known face in the world? Just about everyone recognizes the cheerful image of Colonel Harland Sanders, founder of the Kentucky Fried Chicken empire (now known as KFC). When I met his daughter, Mildred Sanders Ruggles, I learned that some of the "Colonel's" real history is even more colorful than the legends that have grown up about this remarkable man.

First, Colonel Sanders never bought his famous "finger-lickin' good" recipe, nor did he sell it. It was his wife's recipe, to which he added one variation, creating the first "eleven spices and herbs secret recipe." Harland Sanders's first restaurant was an addition to his profitable service station at a busy highway intersection in Kentucky. In 1929, he got the idea of offering home-cooked meals to the truckers who stopped for gas. The whole family pitched in to feed them around a big oak table in their dining room. Because Harland Sanders was scrupulous about quality and service, as well as innovative about food preparation and marketing, his little café prospered and expanded.

One of his earliest innovations was to cut a hole in the wall between the family dining room and kitchen so travelers could see that he owned a refrigerator! In the days before air-conditioning and mandatory food refrigeration, many people feared eating in roadside restaurants in the summertime. Another innovation was to install one of the first electric dishwashers. As the automobile became more and more common, Harland Sanders was among the first to see the potential of "courts," the precursors of the modern motel, with restaurants attached. Despite many setbacks, including a major fire in 1939, he stuck with his Action Plan. KFC now has more than eight thousand locations in fifty-eight countries.

As I talked to the Colonel's charming daughter, she stressed over and over how her father had insisted on performance goals: "He really felt that if you take care of the subtle things—cleanliness, quality, and meeting your customers' needs with a smile—then the business would take care of itself." In other words, concentrate on performance goals, and the outcome goals will follow.

Whether you're building a resilient business or a resilient life, it's the little things that make the big difference. Or as Colonel Sanders himself said, "The easy way is speedy, the hard way arduous and long. [But] the hard way builds a solid foundation of confidence that cannot be swept away."

3. EXPERTISE

Expertise is the third "E" in your goal-seeking process. You've got expectations and an Action Plan, but now you need the know-how.

- What additional knowledge and skills do you need and how can you get them?

- What role models will you choose—people with a track record for achieving what you want to achieve?
- Who can mentor and support your endeavors? How can you involve them in your process?

From Factory Floor to Executive Suite

When ten-year-old Ralph de la Vega got off a plane in Florida, he was all alone and spoke no English. It was 1962, and Ralph's lawyer father was being persecuted by the Castro regime in Cuba. The family planned to emigrate, but at the last minute their visas were withheld. Only young Ralph was free to leave. So his parents made an agonizing decision. They sent him on ahead to stay with friends, hoping to follow him shortly. It was four years before the family was reunited.

Ralph's parents lost everything in the move and had to start over, working in a shoe factory at minimum wage. Ralph supplemented their meager income with jobs after school and on weekends. His goal to attend college seemed out of the question. But Ralph never lost sight of it.

Ralph's first job was cleaning restrooms in a clothing factory. The work was so unpleasant that it made him even more determined to get an education. Soon he was promoted to cleaning the factory floor, then to working in the shipping department. Finally, he found a construction job that paid enough so he could put himself through junior college. He majored in pre-engineering, and, after some drafting courses, he got a job as a draftsman. His wages, combined with a student loan, enabled him to earn a degree in mechanical engineering with honors.

Ralph is currently vice president of consumer services for Bell South in Florida. "Yes, the United States is the land of opportunity!" he says, but clearly Ralph de la Vega made his own opportunities with his personal pursuit of knowledge and excellence.

The only sure way to achieve self-mastery is to invest in your own growth and self-renewal through lifelong learning. Unless we are perpetual students, we risk becoming obsolete in our ever-changing society.

In Chapter 5, you made an inventory of your resources. What skills do you want to acquire or improve? What knowledge do you need? How will you go about obtaining this experience, information, or skill? Incorporate a detailed plan for skill-building in your performance goals.

Teachers and Mentors

Sometimes our teachers also become our mentors or our role models or both. There is a difference. Mentors are people who become our personal boosters, sharing their wisdom and giving us a hand up when needed. Role models are ideals, living or dead. We may never meet them, but their lives are a source of inspiration and a yardstick for measuring our progress.

We need both mentors and role models. When you choose a role model, you can consider every human who has ever lived. When you choose a mentor, you're looking for someone who has the time and energy to invest in you right now. Sometimes mentors choose *you*, but more often you will have to make the first moves, actively cultivating a mentor relationship. Here are the key qualities you're seeking:

- You and your prospective mentor have similar values and integrity.
- The mentor believes in your abilities and is convinced success is possible for you.
- You admire the mentor's achievements, both professional *and* personal. This is extremely important. Some outwardly successful individuals are miserable failures at home. Is this the kind of person you want to model yourself after?
- The mentor sees more in you than you have, so far, seen within yourself. He or she sees you not only as you are, but as you can be.

As a mentoring relationship grows, we develop more ambitious standards for ourselves and try to rise to the expectations of the mentor. Throughout my life, I have emerged from mentoring relationships with deep gratitude. Whenever I am acknowledged for achievements, I am quick to give credit and praise to those who have helped me along the way. Mentors provide the guidance, but you provide the motivation and effort, building your resilience in the process.

Friends in High Places

In the days of vaudeville, performers knew they had made it when they were asked to play the Palace Theatre in New York. Today's professional speakers get the same thrill when they are asked to address the international "Million Dollar Round Table." This organization of top life-insurance salespeople considers more than one thousand speakers each year and chooses just five.

When the selection committee asked me to be the closing speaker in 1986, several people said, "Roger, you must know someone really important to be asked." I did. He was a third-grader from Los Angeles, California.

The year before, I had been hired to do a tour of elementary schools in the Los Angeles area. At one of these assemblies, a youngster in the fifth row seemed very attentive. I demonstrated how I held a tennis racket, and I shared my philosophy about being a positive person, being proud of who you are and aware of what you can be. He hung on every word.

Afterward, this young man asked me a question that no eight-year-old has ever asked me. "Sir," he said, "do you have a business card?" I handed him one. "I'm going to have my daddy call you," he said, "because he hires speakers and I thought you were good." I was astonished, grateful for his belief in me, and impressed by his maturity. I confess that I was also humoring him, never thinking for a moment that this young man could follow through.

About two months later, I received a phone call that I'll never forget: "Roger, this is Michael Ferguson from the Million Dollar Round Table, and if you can hold the attention of a group of elementary-school students for an hour, you can certainly handle our group." Michael had heard of me through Jim Maddux, father of that extraordinary eight-year-old, David Maddux. I closed the 1986 Million Dollar Round Table, speaking to twenty thousand people, and feeling like the entertainer who finally sees his name up in lights at the Palace.

Never overlook opportunities and the help that others can give you. People are often rewarded for personal achievements, but few of us do it alone. Reaching our objectives usually involves the help and inspiration of others. Be sure you cultivate and celebrate the positive relationships in your life.

Continuous Improvement

There is a Japanese word, *Kaizen*, that means "continuous improvement." Or, as strategist Bob Kriegel says, "If it ain't broke, break it." The philosophy of *Kaizen* has been adopted and adapted by many American companies as a way to inspire their employees. The legendary salesman Ben Feldman is a continuous-improvement practitioner. We were scheduled to be on the same speaking platform, and, when I was told that Ben regularly made several million dollars a year selling life insurance, I immediately formed a mental picture of him: tall, attractive, articulate, and immaculately tailored, probably in his mid-fifties. However, when I met Ben in person, I was astonished to find that he did not fit my perception of a superstar salesman. He was in his late seventies, "vertically challenged," his hair was in retreat, and he spoke with a lisp.

But then he began his presentation. He wasn't a skilled speaker and he frequently had to refer to his notes, but his message was so powerful and personal that everyone knew they were in the presence of a giant in the insurance industry. This was even more remarkable when you learn that he had a fear of public speaking so great that he sometimes began speaking from behind a curtain. Nonetheless, he persevered.

When he finished and took questions from the audience, someone asked, "Sir, what is the largest insurance policy you've ever written?" I still remember his answer: "I don't know, I haven't written it yet." Ben Feldman died in his mid-eighties, working to the end. He was the best, and the best always strive to get better.

BOUNCE HIGHER TIP

Concentrate on surpassing your own best performance, not anyone else's.

4. ENDURANCE

Some people have all the enthusiasm and skills necessary for pursuing their ambitions, but they lack the fourth "E"—endurance. They have the talent, the ability, the best strategies, and the right people behind them, but they just can't hang in there. Many people would like to be Olympic champions, but when they discover how much endurance it will take, they give up. Let's face it. Life can be difficult, and to endure, you have to be tougher than a woodpecker's lips.

What motivations for endurance can you create for yourself? Sometimes it takes imagination. When Jim Carrey was a struggling young actor, he wrote himself a check for ten million dollars and postdated it seven years in the future. That check kept him focused, and when it came due, he was able to cover it. Can you design a similarly imaginative strategy that will keep you on track?

Scientists have proven that people (and lab rats!) work longer and harder at tasks if they get a reward now and then. Not a big surprise, perhaps, but an extremely useful tactic to keep in mind. We can help ourselves stay on track toward our objectives by scheduling occasional rewards and periodic celebrations at performance-goal milestones.

Tests also prove that people will stop doing something if they are never rewarded. But the resilient will keep trying long after any self-respecting laboratory rat would have quit. It's this tenacious, wonderfully pig-headed endurance that separates humans from lab animals and provides our opportunities for achieving greatness.

BOUNCE HIGHER TIP

Only imaginary obstacles are insurmountable.

A Window on Endurance

How's this for a daydream: You're standing in your own office, looking out through the window at a range of majestic mountains in the distance. The colors and shadows on the peaks are constantly shifting with the motion of clouds and sun. In this office, you enjoy power and respect, and you're sustained by the beauty and permanence of those mountains. This was the vision of Mike Sanchez.

Mike grew up as one of ten children in a family of migrant farm workers. When he was quite young, his family moved from Texas to the Central Valley of California.

During long days of picking apricots and plums, Mike often stared up at the beautiful Diablo Range mountains in the distance. He told his brother Ray that one day he was going to have an office with a view of those mountains through a large picture window.

Mike was quickly labeled a troublemaker in school, but no one bothered to ask him why he got into so many fights. In fact, Mike was protecting one of his sisters who was born with a cleft lip and palate. When other children ridiculed her, he would rush to her defense. Mike was determined to succeed in school, so he didn't let childhood labels deter him. The way to achieve his window was clearly education, so Mike not only finished high school—already a significant achievement in his community—but he also set his sights on college.

This may sound like a natural progression for a middle-class child with two college-graduate parents and a college fund in the bank since infancy. But try to imagine the enormous challenges it presented for Mike Sanchez. Even with his tremendous personal motivation, the financial obstacles were nearly overwhelming. Mike had to earn scholarships while working at a full-time job. He attended San Jose State University, ultimately completing his masters course work in education. He is currently working toward his doctorate.

The delightful payoff of this story is that when Mike was appointed principal of San Andreas High School, the new building stood on the site where Mike had picked fruit as a child. That's right! The window of his office now overlooks those same mountains he gazed at as a young boy.

San Andreas High School is a continuation school for students who have been having a wide variety of difficulties. Sometimes a student comes into Mike's office, really down in the dumps, and says, "I'm a loser. I'll never get anywhere." Mike told me that he usually puts his arm around the youngster's shoulders and suggests they take a walk outside. As they stand in the parking lot, he points to the mountains in the distance. Then he tells the story of a young boy who looked at those mountains years ago and dreamed of seeing them through his office window.

"I try to get them to believe what I believe," Mike says. "That it doesn't matter what color you are or what shape you are, and it doesn't matter where you've come from. What matters is that you know where you're *going!*"

5. EVALUATION

It's the traditional American dream: If you set a goal and work hard enough, you'll succeed. This is a reality for many, but there are no guarantees. Without periodic evaluation of your progress, without checking for course corrections, it's easy to get off track. And if you don't pause to evaluate, how will you know when you've reached your goal?

> ### BOUNCE HIGHER TIP
>
> *If you don't periodically ask, "Where am I going?"*
> *the groove you're in can become a rut.*

Some people confuse activity with creativity, and movement with achievement. They think that busy-ness and living at a hectic pace equal output. Other want to arrive without making the journey. They dream of glory but are unwilling to make the effort.

Keep a time chart or graph to record your progress. As you design your Action Plan, be sure it has built-in reality checks. Schedule periodic evaluations and prepare an evaluation questionnaire specific to your goals. Your questions might include:

- Am I on schedule? If not:
    Was my original timetable too optimistic?
    Have unforeseen factors affected it?
    Do I need to rethink my strategies?
    Do I need more resources? (Knowledge, advice, outside support?)
- Has my ultimate goal shifted because of new insights and information? If so, what changes should I make?
- What will be different when I reach my objective?
- Where exactly is the finish line? How will I know when I've reached it?

Block Busters

What if your evaluation reveals that you've gotten stuck? If, despite your best efforts, you're still unsuccessful, try these block-buster techniques:

Acknowledge your roadblock. Use resilient thinking: "Yes, I'm blocked, and I have four choices. I can go around it, through it, over it, or I can use this barrier as a launching pad." Visualize yourself swimming laps with the obstacle as the end of the pool. When you reach it, you can clunk into it headfirst, or you can turn and use it to push yourself off at even higher speed. Or get outside help. Notice that everyone you've ever met or heard about has also encountered obstructions. Then read about other people's experiences, or seek out someone who has run into a tough spot and struggled successfully against the impediment.

Remind yourself where you are coming from. Credit yourself for past perseverance by identifying instances in your past when you've overcome obstacles. Relive those victories for renewed endurance.

Remind yourself where you're going. Can you make yourself view your current block as a challenge rather than a disaster? Remember that life would lack richness if we never had to struggle. Try to put blocks in perspective, seeing them as opportunities for building character and resilience. Visualize this experience as a deposit in your resilience account.

Find something to make you laugh. At our house, you might be surprised to hear someone saying, "Listen to the pig." The pig in question is bright pink and stuffed. It oinks and says "I love you" whenever you get near it, and it keeps this up until you walk away. When my daughter, Alexa, gets tired and whiny, we sometimes suggest a visit to the pig. Alexa has taken this lesson to heart because one day, when I'd had several disappointments, she advised me, "Listen to the pig, Daddy." I laughed so hard that it was impossible to feel down. Several corporate clients of mine have heard this story and gotten similar pigs for the desks of their staff members. Find a "pet" of your own that makes you laugh and releases that spirit of mental energy. Then go back and bust your block.

Three Myths About Goals

Laurels are impressive, but they can be uncomfortable to rest on for too long. Once we've reached our goals and objectives, we can savor the victory for only a short time. Then it's time to move on. Don't let these myths about success rob you of your real triumph.

Myth #1—Success brings happiness.
Fact #1—Success brings a sense of achievement along with new challenges.

Even when our achievements exactly match our goals, we can go into a sort of "postpartum depression." All that effort, and now it's over. All of us have experienced this. We were sure that a victory or achievement would change our lives and make us feel terrific. Then, when we succeeded, we experienced a letdown, no matter what we'd accomplished.

So we all have two choices. Either we can never pursue goals, or we can decide to have realistic expectations about how we'll feel and how others will feel about us when we have reached our goals.

When we define ourselves as achievers who get satisfaction from both the journey and the destination, we ensure contentment, satisfaction, and a sense of fulfillment when we reach a goal.

Each objective achieved is something we will always be proud of and draw strength from, but the contentment soon wanes. It's time to try something new, to create new incentives. This restlessness is the key to human achievement. The resilient achievers I've observed have all been able to enjoy each victory fully and then move on without regret. Their desire for growth and mastery propels them forward as they set themselves new and more difficult tasks.

Myth #2—"I must not fail."
Fact #2—"I will screw up royally from time to time, and I'm prepared for this."

Now and then, external factors and our own failings are going to knock us off course. Some of these detours will be beyond our control. We didn't know, we didn't anticipate, we didn't understand.

When you are setting goals, remember that the results you'll achieve are inevitably a combination of controllable and uncontrollable forces. Learn from the controllable ones. Accept and compensate for the uncontrollable ones. Extract the information relevant to your future actions, and then look ahead. "I must not fail" is nonresilient thinking, emphasizing the negative. "I'm prepared" is resilient thinking, focusing on the positive.

Myth #3—"Once I succeed, that's it."
Fact #3—"Once I succeed, my work is just starting."

When Jack Canfield was developing his book, *Chicken Soup for the Soul*, he focused on making it the best book possible. He was sure that if he succeeded, the book would fly off the bookstore shelves. The day the books were finally shipped to the bookstores, he sat in his chair, visualizing crowds standing in line to grab the books, and thinking about how his life would change. What happened? Nothing. "It was the calm before the calm," he recalls.

Then Jack realized that only part of his work was done. *He* knew he had an outstanding book, but other people didn't. He had to be proactive and let them know. He learned how to market his book, giving TV and radio interviews and writing dozens of articles. His marketing campaign (plus the quality of his book) have made *Chicken Soup for the Soul* a best-seller, with more than eight million copies sold.

Often we fool ourselves into thinking that, once we've accomplished something, our work is done and we'll automatically advance to another level. More often our work is just beginning.

P R O F I L E
Larry Bird

As my car approached the city limits of French Lick, Indiana, I felt a sudden rush of excitement. Few people have heard of French Lick, and fewer still have been there. Unless you're an avid basketball fan like I am. French Lick is the birthplace of one of the most phenomenal athletes that ever stepped on a basketball court, Larry Bird.

Larry Legend, as many call him, is admired worldwide for his tenacity, audacity, and ability to achieve greatness at every level of competition. Now I was in French Lick to make a speech, and I had a chance to find out the childhood influences that had helped to form Larry Bird's incredible resilience.

My host was Roger Fisher, assistant superintendent of the Paoli schools. During a break in my presentation, I asked Roger if he knew Larry Bird. Roger chuckled. "My claim to fame is that I was Larry Bird's eighth-grade coach," he said, "and I kicked him off the team!"

I had to know why. As we talked, I learned some facts that few people know about Larry's early life. He was the third of six children, five boys and one girl. His father was chronically unemployed and an alcoholic who ultimately took his own life when Larry was in high school. Larry's mother was a strong, proud woman who held her family together, often working at three jobs. The family was close-knit and devoted to one another. If one of the children was ridiculed for wearing shabby clothes, the others would leap to his or her defense. Larry learned early about teamwork and the need to rely on others.

As early as junior high school, his love of basketball was obvious. Coach Fisher told me that Larry was simultaneously very aggressive and very shy. He was so determined to be the best that he'd stay for hours after a game, practicing over and over the shots he'd missed during the contest. Ironically, this tenacity and perfectionism also stood in Larry's way. He was so passionate to achieve that he was unable to control his temper under pressure. This led to a series of angry outbursts on the basketball court during his eighth-grade year.

One day Coach Fisher had to tell Larry that he'd gone too far and could no longer be on the team. Larry was devastated. Basketball meant everything to him. However, this jolt made him reevaluate his attitude toward achievement. He finally accepted that we can be committed to excellence and still tolerate imperfections in ourselves and others. He refocused his energies on new goals and made the team again, becoming a star on the Spring Valley High School team.

Larry's next big challenge was going off to college. He got a scholarship at Indiana University, a source of great pride for the whole town of French Lick. To come from a small town and play for the legendary coach Bobby Knight made Larry a local hero.

Then came another setback. Larry quickly felt out of place at the university. French Lick had a total population of two thousand people, and the university had thirty thousand students. The experience was overwhelming for a small-town boy. After just a month, Larry became so homesick that he left school. His inability to achieve his goal saddened everyone in French Lick.

Larry's life took another turn that no one associates with Hall of Famers. He went to work as a garbage collector. Most others in a similar situation would say, "Well, I had my chance and I blew it. The rest of my life will be like this." But Larry Legend still burned to be an NBA champion.

A year later, he enrolled at the lesser-known Indiana State. Larry led their basketball team to the NCAA finals, where they lost to Michigan State, led by Magic Johnson. Larry went on to join the Boston Celtics and to become a National Basketball Association and Olympic basketball champion. He was voted Most Valuable Player several times. He had an uncanny ability to hit the winning shot and was considered one of the greatest "pressure players" in the NBA. Today, he's the head coach of the Indiana Pacers.

Resilient lives have their own rhythms. Larry Bird's life shows us that we can endure failure and still go on to achieve our goals. He was tossed off the eighth-grade basketball team and he dropped out of college, but neither setback kept him down. Larry Bird continued to define his ultimate purpose so vividly that nothing could stop him.

R E S I L I E N C E   B U I L D E R

Harnessing the Power of Purpose

If you already follow a regular program of setting objectives and monitoring your progress, congratulations. Use these resilience builders to reinforce your plan. And if you haven't started yet, or you're not getting the results you'd like to get, use the following guidelines to focus yourself.

1. Forging Your Vision

- Dream big. Resilient people manage to be hard-nosed realists about the details while, at the same time, being visionary about their lives. Reach into the treasure chest of your mind for those childlike fantasies of what you'd like to be and do and share. Visualize the people, feelings, and places you want to be part of your life.
- Define your dream and write a vision statement. Then look at what you've written. Do the ideas stir and galvanize your heart and soul? Do they mobilize and inspire you? Most important, do they mirror your value system?

2. Achieving Your Goals

- Design specific objectives that will move you toward your goals. Add supporting goals that seem important to you.

Then look at your list. If the tasks that energize and excite you aren't those that support your goal statement, do some serious reevaluating. You may need to write a new one.

- Make a comprehensive list of the most important resources you already possess. Decide which of them will support your goals.
- Focus on several successful occasions in your life and remember what you did to achieve that success. What qualities and resources did you use? Will they be useful now?
- Write a description of the type of person you will have to be to reach your highest aspirations. What beliefs will you have to have? What skills? What attitudes will you have to develop or reinforce? What behaviors, if any, will you have to change or strengthen?
- Describe your destination clearly. Have a powerful mental picture of what your arrival looks like.
- Troubleshoot. What has been keeping you from reaching your highest ambitions? Identify and evaluate your limitations.
- Make a timetable. Decide on specific time lines and lifelines, rather than deadlines. Break your plan into manageable parts, from yearly all the way down to what you can do daily to further your efforts. Build in rewards and reevaluations.

The Poetry of Goals

My teen years were spent in the San Francisco Bay Area, so naturally I was an ardent Oakland Raiders fan. The "Silver and Black" were one of the top National Football League teams at the time. Pete Banaszak, Gene Upshaw, and Dave Casper were all my heroes, but my favorite player was "the Snake," left-handed quarterback Ken Stabler.

Once Ken was being interviewed by a reporter who was an admirer of Jack London, author of *The Call of the Wild* and other rugged adventure stories. In pursuit of an inspiring quote, the reporter read aloud this poem by London:

I would rather be ashes than dust!
I would rather
That my spark should burn out in a brilliant blaze
Than that it should be stifled by dry rot.
I would rather be a superb meteor,
Every atom of me in magnificent glow,
Than a sleepy and permanent planet.
The proper function of man is to live, not to exist.
I shall not waste my days in trying to prolong them.
I shall use my time.

The reporter paused to let these words stir Stabler's soul. Then he asked him, "What do these words mean to you?"

Ken Stabler replied, in his lilting Alabama accent, "Seems to me he's saying, 'Always throw deep.' "

8

Develop Your Inborn Leadership

SHARE YOUR VISION

It's probably happened to you too—one of those frustrating flights to nowhere. My family and I were at the Albuquerque airport, eager to get home to San Francisco. At the check-in counter, we discovered numerous people milling about, looking upset. The plane had been delayed because of mechanical problems. We were tired, but we understood. I'm always grateful when an airline takes the time to fix mechanical problems. (When the person behind the counter asks, "Would you like a window, a middle, or an aisle seat?" I relieve any anxiety I might have by replying, "Just put me in the black box, please.")

The delay stretched on and on. Four hours later, we were allowed to board. The plane backed up about ten feet and stopped. Then it returned to the gate, and the pilot apologized, "Ladies and gentlemen, I'm terribly sorry, but I must cancel this flight."

Many around us were ranting and raving about the meetings they would miss and the urgency of reaching their destinations.

Back inside the terminal, people were shouting furiously at the boarding clerk, "I'm never going to fly this airline again!" One man said, "Why can't you fly even though the brakes are bad?" Apparently he didn't care about the landing at the other end, as long as he got there. I knew it wasn't the clerk's fault and I calmly arranged for another flight the next day.

As I turned from the counter, a man approached me. "I heard you speak at my company this morning," he said, "and I've been watching you for the last four hours. You told us about responding positively to negative situations, and I just wanted to see if you lived what you preach. Thanks for not disappointing me."

What a wake-up call! This made me reflect on other occasions when I may not have acted so positively. It also made me aware that we're all constantly being observed by others—by our families, our colleagues, our clients, and complete strangers—and that each of us leads primarily by example.

You are a leader, even if you don't always think of yourself that way. You have many followers. Every time you exhibit resilience, you awaken others to their own resilient potential. You are demonstrating your inborn leadership abilities and spreading a wide net of influence and power.

The Resilient Leader

Every effective leader offers two fundamentals: a course of action and positive feelings. Each is valuable by itself, but together they make an unbeatable combination. To persuade and inspire others, start by communicating your own optimistic resilience and showing others how they can develop it.

Resilience is both attractive and contagious. It's the leader who ultimately sets the tone for the entire organization, and people are drawn to the leader who stimulates their own resilience and inspires hope. The most popular recent presidents have been those who boosted the hope level of the nation.

BOUNCE HIGHER TIP

Become a "heart specialist."
Listen to the heartbeats of those you lead.

Not everyone in a position of power is a leader, and not all leaders have fully developed their own resilience. From my observations of more than two thousand different companies around the world that have faced a variety of challenges and changes, I've concluded that people at the top generally fall into two categories.

Traditional Leaders	*Resilient Leaders*
Issue orders	**Share a vision**
• Set goals	• Inspire achievement
• Enforce rules and regulations	• Guide and overcome resistance by sharing values
• Change in response to crisis	• Reinterpret change and crisis to maximize learning and innovation
• Establish authority	• Earn trust
Exert authority	**Coach and encourage**
• Are bosses	• Are guides
• Set limits	• Expand horizons
• Value results only	• Value quality, flexibility, and persistence, as well as results

Control	Empower
• Guard their power	• Confer power
• Are independent	• Are interdependent
• Say "My way or the highway"	• Delegate, cultivate, and unify

I'm enormously grateful for good managers. They keep the wheels turning, meet goals, and save us time and energy. They can even stimulate us to feel like a valuable part of the team and to work harder than we've ever worked before. But management isn't leadership. A manager's job is to produce better goods and services. A leader's job is to produce better people.

True leadership goes beyond efficiency. It helps us answer the big question, "Where are you going?" It provides a vision of where we can go and what we can accomplish. Then it stimulates us to act. For a limited time, we can stay fairly productive without leadership, just as we can keep going on coffee and junk food. But sooner or later we need more.

Many experts agree that we have been over-managed and under-led. Too many managers confuse quotas with inspiration and deadlines with motivation. They may imagine themselves in the forefront, carrying the banner, but they're actually in the back, cracking the whip. The troops are driven rather than led.

True leaders have qualities that make them inspiring to watch: boldness, courage, passion, vision, integrity, a sense of adventure, and a high energy level, all characteristics of resilience. True leaders take more than their share of the blame and less than their share of the credit. They have a realistic idea of their own competencies, what they can do well and what they do less well. They acknowledge and compensate for their shortcomings while nurturing their strengths and applying them effectively. And what is the result of being a strong, effective, resilient leader? As a number of top executives have told me, you can tell good leaders because at some point their followers will determine they are no longer needed. The ultimate tribute.

Although we can never "make" someone resilient, we can all help others to grow their own supply of resilience. How?

SHARE YOUR VISION

No great thing is ever done by someone without a vision. Ideas may be nothing without action, but action is empty without a vision. Convert your dreams into goals and your goals into visions. A goal is something you wrap your mind around. A vision is something you wrap your heart around. Goals are definable, measurable, and objective. Vision is unquantifiable and a unique expression of who you are. Goals are right-brain. Vision is left-brain. Goals are practical. Vision stirs the passions and exhilarates the soul.

Goals are almost always less ambitious than visions. When we set goals, we usually strive for something attainable, something within our reach as we see it. Our visions, on the other hand, inspire us and everyone around us to struggle beyond our perceived limitations. They can help us to reach objectives that we never thought possible.

Resilient people are simultaneously down-to-earth pragmatists and pie-in-the-sky dreamers. The French mathematician René Descartes wrote of a "fiery angel" who suddenly appeared to him in the night, revealing the answers to questions he had been pondering. We all have access to these fiery angels of insight and inspiration. The challenge is to harness the energy of our visions and then to share them with others.

BOUNCE HIGHER TIP

To lead others, offer both a clear finish line and an exciting vision of how things will be afterward.

Without vision, goals can sometimes actually be counter-productive. We can bog down in details and narrow our focus until we lose sight of the big picture. For instance, let's say that you set a goal of getting a particular contract as part of a larger professional vision, but then you get so preoccupied with competing for the contract that you fail to notice changing business factors that make the goal obsolete. Or you fail to get the contract and then are at a loss about what to do next.

Both self-leadership and the influencing of millions need the boost of the big picture.

An entrepreneur named William Jaird Levitt had such an image. In the population boom after World War II, returning GI's faced an acute housing shortage. However, the price for building a new home was far beyond the reach of all but a few. Then Levitt decided that the cost of individual houses could be kept rock-bottom if an entire community was built at once. His vision, translated into practical goals, produced Levittown, New York; Levittown, New Jersey; and Levittown, Pennsylvania. Levitt lived to see countless similar communities of affordable housing arise across America, inspired by his example. Because of his vision, a generation of Americans grew up in their own homes.

Vision provides the essential overview and the energy to keep everyone going when they run into roadblocks. It's the catalyst for reaching our full potential.

The Visionary Inspires Achievement

At an international conference on communications technology, one of the world's leading trend predictors stood up to speak. Representatives of dozens of Fortune 500 companies leaned forward, eager to hear how the latest advances could benefit their organizations.

Yet, when Sukij Yongpiyakul launched into his speech, he did not begin with a spellbinding view of technological miracles to come. Instead, he told the audience, "In business today, if I had one dollar to spend, I'd spend it inspiring my people, not buying technology. Our world is changing so rapidly that the moment you buy technology, it starts depreciating. But an investment in inspiration and empowerment of people invariably appreciates. Never forget that 'heart-ware' is more important than hardware."

Inspiration and motivation aren't identical. Resilient leaders must deal with both, so it helps to know the difference. When you inspire, you touch the *internal,* arousing feelings and emotions. When you motivate, you stir the *external* and stimulate physical action. When you excite people to respond both internally and externally, you are a true leader.

The Visionary Guides with Shared Values

Suppose a boss demands that his employees be on time, but is frequently late. Suppose a mother and father tell their children how important it is to be honest, and then brag about the speed-trap detector in their car. Or about getting "extra" change at the supermarket or taking false income-tax deductions. What kind of messages are they sending? For the resilient leader, actions and words must match. Model the behavior you expect.

Before you can hope to lead others, you have to establish a high level of trust and shared values. Trust in those at the top is integral to a resilient organization. Such trust doesn't show up on a balance sheet, but it is an asset beyond price. People may admire you for your skill, charm, or knowledge, but they *trust* you for two reasons:

Flexible consistency. During my travels, I've heard many people describe their leaders in almost the same words: "We may disagree, but I know where s/he stands." This means that the leader's words and actions match, and that a clear, consistent vision guides the leader's actions. Notice that I said *flexible* consistency. Followers want to follow a clear path, but they'll readily accept changes in direction from a leader they trust, one who listens and responds.

Self-discipline. Managers do things right. Leaders do the right things. Resilient leaders identify what needs to be done and have the self-discipline to take action. They are masters of self-control and believe that high ethics are not optional. They know how to hang in there when times are tough.

Any organization that is going to navigate turbulent times needs resilient leaders that people can trust, leaders who demonstrate consistency and discipline. Sometimes a leader must make a difficult and painful decision, but followers will accept it and trust that it is the right decision if they trust their leader. Trust is the lifeblood of resilient organizations.

The Visionary Overcomes Resistance

What could be more disconcerting for a leader than looking around and discovering that no one is following? Or even worse, finding that everyone is running in the opposite direction? When this happens, it takes extra resilience to persist in your vision.

One man who persevered is Don Petty, a construction specialist with The St. Paul Companies, a Fortune 500 company in Minnesota. His job is to decide what safety procedures are needed on job sites insured by St. Paul. When a 150-foot-high atrium was under construction, he strongly recommended using safety nets. The customer and contractor agreed, but before the starting date, they changed their minds, insisting that individual safety harnesses would be sufficient.

The visionary leader must be able to foresee potential problems as well as future successes. Don Petty stood his ground, refusing to sign off on the project until the nets were installed. During the following six months, thirteen workers survived falls because of the nets. Don Petty's vision saved St. Paul three million dollars in insurance claims, and, far more important, his resilience saved thirteen lives.

The Visionary Reinterprets Change and Crisis

Few things separate resilient leaders from traditional leaders more than their ability to inspire themselves and others to learn and grow during setbacks. Here are three of their key skills:

Find positive labels for setbacks. Nearly every "failure" can be interpreted as a positive experience, even if it's only as a barometer to show what needs improvement and where we are progressing and learning. People may not be able to see this when they have just suffered a major disappointment. But when enough time has passed to allow perspective, the leader asks what can be learned from the experience.

BOUNCE HIGHER TIP

Leading yourself out of failure is often easier than leading sustained success.

Separate setbacks. When several bad events happen at about the same time, it's easy for the less-resilient to see them as proof of a perpetual continuum of failure and inadequacy. Help others to view each negative event separately. Point out, when this is true, that each event had a completely different cause, and that they are not related.

Reinterpret setbacks as challenges. When the initial pain and frustration have passed, explore whether this setback has suggested any new challenges. Never try to tell others what you think these challenges are. Guide gently and wait patiently until they can discover them for themselves so that they "own" them.

FOUR VISIONARY QUESTIONS

- "How far do you think you want to go right now?" *(Create a strong vision of the next few years.)*
- "How will achieving this vision make things better for the group?" *(Promote a sense of self-worth by relating personal progress to potential benefits to others.)*
- "What would be the best way to help you get there?" *(Sensitivity to personal perceptions makes you an ally in his or her advancement.)*
- "When you achieve this, what will you tackle next?" *(Show that you already recognize their potential to do more and be more.)*

COACH AND ENCOURAGE

Think of the last time you watched a child trying to get the attention of an adult, shouting, "Watch me! Watch me!" Throughout our lives, we all say this. Perhaps not out loud, but always in our hearts. Imagine an invisible sign on everyone's chest: "Watch me! Make me feel important!" Develop the habit of noticing and reflecting back people's value and effort. Any leader that can achieve this heads a powerful organization.

How do you prove to your team members that they are special? The recognition can range from encouraging words and supportive internal structures to a formal award or ceremony. It doesn't have to take a lot of time or elaborate strategies. For example, the sales staff at Ingram Micro, a billion-dollar company and leading distributor of computer software and hardware, were astonished to look out the window one day and see their president, Jeff Rodek, hard at work in the parking lot. Without telling anyone, he'd decided to wash all their cars to show how much he appreciated their efforts. It was a morale builder that people talked about for months.

You can't overestimate the value of making people feel a vital part of the whole. Recently, I was due at Gateway Data Sciences of Phoenix. "Shall I let the receptionist know I've arrived?" I asked. "Oh, we don't have a receptionist," the executive replied. I was really puzzled. How did such a successful company function without someone to direct visitors? "No," continued the executive, "we have a Director of First Impressions. You can check in with her." When I arrived and chatted with this Director, I discovered that she felt empowered by her title, valued, and had a strong sense of contributing to Gateway's progress.

Resilient leaders—whether they're inspiring a family or a nation—keep their organizations elastic and strong by promoting respect and pride at every level. In such an environment, everyone is able to perform at his or her best.

One of the most effective leaders I've ever met was my school-bus driver, Mrs. Torchianna. The president has to deal with Congress. A CEO may deal with hundreds of regional managers and a hundred thousand employees. Their accomplishments pale before the prospect of handling a bus full of active fourth graders. Maneuvering a bulky, awkward bus through traffic requires absolute concentration and focus. Add seventy-five screaming voices, a few flying apples, and an upset stomach or two, and you'll start to respect Mrs. Torchianna's masterful leadership. How did she do it?

Mrs. Torchianna had such an infectious smile, even the grumpy kids had to smile back. The first day you boarded her bus, she asked you your name and she never forgot it. Each morning it was, "Hello, Roger. Hello, Marybelle. I hope you're having a good day today." And as she drove us on our way, she would sing to us.

Mrs. Torchianna never forgot a student's birthday. She wrote it down on a chalkboard that she'd attached to the back of her seat. Then, as the birthday child boarded the bus, she would signal to the other students, and everyone would begin singing "Happy Birthday." It was something that we all looked forward to.

She kept us more or less under control with a very effective reward system. Every Friday, she baked some large and very delicious chocolate-chip cookies. These were kept in a brown paper sack beside her seat. We'd ride home Friday afternoon, smelling those cookies. If you had behaved during the week, you got a cookie as you exited the bus.

Needless to say, no one moved a muscle on Friday. We had the best-behaved school bus in town, and it was all because of Mrs. Torchianna's leadership style. She was enthusiastic, positive, disciplined, and encouraged us to be our best. Most of all, she made everyone feel important.

The Coach Expands Horizons

Despite all the talk about the importance of "motivating people," no one can really motivate someone else. The best we can do is provide the right triggers for self-motivation. There are some popular and generally successful buttons to push, but nothing is guaranteed to work with every person every time. We're all motivated by different things on different occasions. Effective leaders use their sensitivity to find out what makes particular people act. Then they speak to that need.

In today's increasingly diverse world, a resilient leader learns to evaluate people in terms of both performance and *potential*. The best leaders are those who can see beyond what someone is now to what they could become. These leaders don't just hire high-performance people, they "grow" them. Anyone who stays behind a door with a brass nameplate can't hope to develop this kind of sensitivity.

Sensitive communication means listening for the meaning behind the words. One of Stephen Covey's seven habits in his book, *The 7 Habits of Highly Effective People,* is "Seek first to understand, then to be understood." He adds, "We have such a tendency to rush in, to fix things up with good advice. But we often fail to take the time to diagnose, to really, deeply understand the problem first."

For example, in one rural community, the town council was eager to improve the grades and reduce the high absenteeism and dropout rate of children from an isolated area. The council members considered raising the school budget to buy computers and sports equipment, hiring special tutors, or increasing funds for truant officers, even extra police to prevent petty disturbances caused by the out-of-school youngsters. Finally, one council member had the good sense to talk to the children themselves to find out why they seemed so unmotivated. She might have been discouraged by their first replies: "We hate school!" most cried. Fortunately, she listened beyond these words. She discovered that many were ashamed to go to school, because they were often put down by their classmates for turning up unbathed and in dirty clothes. This was not a lack of desire for cleanliness on their part, but rather a lack of running water and electricity in their homes. (Imagine chopping ice and boiling it to bathe in the dead of winter!) The city council decided to extend power and utility services to their area, and school attendance promptly increased.

How sensitive are you to the real needs of others? Do you ever catch yourself concentrating so hard on what you want to say next that you have no idea what the other person is saying? Can you listen past the words to the real meaning?

The Coach Values Persistence

Don't jump in to save those you care about from the struggle of life's experiences. One of the biggest mistakes we can make is to tell someone, "Don't bother. I'll do it for you." Often the listener hears the message, "You aren't competent to accomplish this."

Start by trusting others to learn on their own. This doesn't mean you don't share expectations, goals, guidelines, and a powerful arsenal of resources to draw on. It doesn't mean you leave others to sink or swim. And it doesn't mean that you don't offer support and sympathy when honest effort fails.

Ultimately, how people respond to new challenges depends on how they view the failures and triumphs of their past ("Where Are You Coming From?"). They need to go through the process to acquire these experiences.

> I hear—I understand.
> I do—I learn.
> I feel—I change.

If someone has always rescued them or come along after them to "fix" things, they have no model for succeeding in the future. Even repeated failures can teach resilience. It is within these experiences that we discover our stamina and resources.

FOUR COACHING QUESTIONS

- "How would you like to handle this?" *(Encourage others to find their own solutions, and assist them with outside supports if they need them.)*
- "How else could we achieve this?" *(Share what you know and urge others to contribute too.)*
- "On a scale of one to ten, how are you doing right now?" *(Invite a self-evaluation that leads to a realistic discussion of performance level.)*
- "What's the best way to resolve this setback? What's worked in the past?" *(Introduce the language of resilience as a learning tool.)*

EMPOWER

Resilient people feel they have control. Fortunately, it is usually possible to "work backward," building resilience by giving someone a sense of control. It was this kind of "empowerment" that made the Saturn one of the most sought-after cars in America. By the mid-1990s, Saturn had been rated third in customer satisfaction four years in a row, surpassed only by two luxury imports. Ignoring traditional automotive quality-control programs, Saturn management decided that anyone working on the assembly line could stop production at any time if he or she felt there was a problem that needed fixing. This sense of control translated into enormous pride of workmanship for Saturn employees and superior cars coming off the assembly line.

BOUNCE HIGHER TIP

Whenever possible, offer options and invite others to come up with their own.

Resilient leaders have the self-assurance to let go of some control. Resilient leadership today includes delegating and giving followers the chance to make mistakes. All of us become more involved, creative, responsible, and responsive when we feel we have some influence. The more input, the higher the level of performance and productivity and the stronger the organization. Leaders fearful of sacrificing power often ignore such input, forgetting that the people closest to the situation usually have the most knowledge about how to handle it best.

The Empowerer Promotes Interdependence

The team concept sometimes takes a beating in our star-oriented culture, yet we all need to be on at least one team. The family/community team has been the primary social unit for thousands of years, but when it breaks down, the need for belonging is so fundamental that young people create their own teams. The police call these teams gangs.

While a good coach can build teams and team spirit, an empowerer goes one step further, giving others a sense of control over their lives and their destinies. Good leaders never forget to communicate that they're also part of the team.

The Honcho and the Hamburger

Some CEO's at corporate events are like comets. Their imminent arrival is well publicized and eagerly awaited. They swoop in on the dot, make a big impression, and then scoot out a side door and vanish.

Not Bill Marriott, whose family name has become synonymous with hotels. I was honored to find myself at the same table with him at a General Managers' Meeting in Orlando, Florida. He immediately impressed me by how accessible he is to his employees, and by his sharp memory. I sat in awe as he greeted people by name and asked about their jobs and families, even if he hadn't seen them for some time.

The year before had been a record one for his hotel chain. I was sure Bill Marriott was going to emphasize this financial success to the 650 men and women in the room. That's why I'll never forget his first words: "Marriott is about people . . . people make the difference."

Then Bill Marriott told a wonderful story about one of his employees, a man called Smitty. Smitty is the room-service captain at the Atlanta Downtown Marriott. He is also an avid baseball fan. Naturally Smitty was enormously proud that the Major League Baseball teams stayed at the Marriott when they came to Atlanta to play the Braves. He's a very jovial person and got to know many of the ballplayers and managers.

Then another major chain hotel was built nearby, and it began wooing the Major League Baseball teams by offering them substantial discounts. About half the teams switched to this less-expensive hotel.

Smitty decided to win them back. "Whenever a team that wasn't staying at the Marriott came to town, I took the day off. I'd . . . find out what time the team was scheduled to arrive. Then I'd go over in full uniform and wait for the team in th[eir] lobby. One time the Dodgers came to town. Tommy Lasorda led the team into the [rival hotel], and I was standing there waiting for him. . . . 'I just wanted to welcome you to town, wish you good luck against the Braves, and tell you that I'm bringing over your special order of hamburgers and french fries from Marriott after the game tonight.' [This was in the days before Lasorda began advertising a diet drink.]

"He asked me why I would do such a thing, and I told him that [this hotel's] room service closes at eleven P.M.—if the game went extra innings, he'd miss his late-night snack. 'But more importantly,' I said, 'I just want you to know that even though you can't afford to stay with us anymore, we still love you.' "

At 12:15 that night, Smitty personally delivered Lasorda's favorite snack, specially prepared by the Marriott kitchen. Lasorda was so impressed that he told Peter O'Malley, the team's general manager. Eventually, because of personal attention like this, all the Major League teams switched back to the Marriott.

In some organizations, someone acting autonomously like Smitty might have been reprimanded or even fired. Not at Marriott. Bill Marriott believes that everyone is a potential leader, and he sees that this philosophy is conveyed down the chain of command. All Bill's employees are empowered to act.

The Empowerer Unifies and Delegates

What was the last time you felt excited and totally involved with a project? Was it because you had luxurious surroundings, a great medical plan, or a fancy title? Probably not.

Some leaders think they can improve loyalty just by providing luxurious premises and generous benefits. However, "things" are rarely good motivators. The resilient leader knows that people can perform magnificently under highly stressful conditions if they possess esprit de corps. This loyalty and enthusiasm results when leaders are sensitive to the true needs of their followers: a sense of personal growth, of achievement, and of being essential to the success of a group that is performing an important task.

Resilient leaders can keep groups of people on track toward a common goal even when their individual needs are in conflict. Too often, disagreements represent *perceived* needs for recognition, concern, protection, or comfort. By listening and getting feedback, a resilient leader can often resolve conflicts by providing what is really needed, not what is asked for.

FOUR EMPOWERING QUESTIONS

- "What needs to be done? How? When?" (*Get others to invest in the project.*)
- "What should we expect from you?" (*Jointly establish expectations and standards.*)
- "What's going to be different in the future?" (*Involve others in anticipating and preparing for change.*)
- "Who are you counting on? Who is depending on you? How?" (*Demonstrate interconnectedness.*)

Leading the Next Generation

On a flight to Bakersfield, I fell into conversation with a champion equestrian, Anita Simpson, who was on her way to a rodeo. She remarked that training a horse is exactly like training a child. As a father, I was intrigued but skeptical.

She explained that she had just been working with a horse that had been trained with a heavyweight bit. When she put her standard lightweight-metal bit into its mouth, the horse failed to recognize her commands. "But if you start them off with a lightweight bit, the horse gets used to responding to the lightest touch. Eventually you can use something as light as a shoestring and the horse responds instantly. It's the same with children," she concluded. "If you train them with shouting, they won't obey whispers."

Isn't that how we want to lead those most important to us? With the lightest touch and by example? Leading giant corporations and governments may be important, but there is one leadership responsibility that surpasses both. Our ultimate task as resilient leaders is to lead our own children. How can we, as a nation, give our children the resilience they need to survive and thrive? To find out what makes a resilient child, psychologist Bonnie Benard compiled the results of dozens of studies to come up with some general conclusions. One bright spot was the discovery that some children seem able to recover from deprivation and abuse: "Half of the children living under conditions of disadvantage do not repeat that pattern in their own adult lives."

According to Benard, highly resilient children shared five qualities, the same qualities that enable all children to thrive.

People who come from difficult backgrounds may worry that they won't be able to provide what their children need, but fortunately these five essential qualities have nothing to do with purchasing power. And they can all be taught or at least encouraged.

- **Social Competence**—Resilient children are responsive, flexible, and caring; they have good communication skills and a sense of humor.

- **Problem-Solving Skills**—Resilient kids work hard to figure out difficult situations and to come up with alternate solutions. They plan ahead.

- **Autonomy**—Also called "a strong sense of independence," "internal locus of control," "a sense of power," "self-esteem," "self-efficacy," "self-discipline," and "impulse control." At a very early age, resilient children are able to decide that they are not the cause of their parents' problems, and that their own future can and will be entirely different.

- **A Sense of Purpose and Future**—A strong vision of how life can and should be protects at-risk children from taking the path of least resistance. High expectations are apparently both a cause and an effect of childhood resilience.

- **One Close Personal Relationship**—A close bond with at least one other person, not necessarily their father or mother, is a key component of a child's resilience. In the earliest years, the child was provided with stable and adequate care and attention by this person.

How we communicate with our children may be the most critical leadership challenge we'll ever face. Here are some guidelines.

Use the Language of Resilience. As parents and teachers, one of the most valuable messages we can give them is that it's okay to make mistakes. Let your kids know that if something doesn't turn out well, it may simply be another way of doing things. Nothing is a complete failure if it is a learning experience that brings them another step closer to accomplishment.

Label Behavior, Not People. After an educational conference, I was chatting with a group of teaching professionals about their work and the structure of their schools. One teacher told me about a second-grade class she had recently taken over from another teacher who had had limited success with the children. When the new teacher arrived, she found that her predecessor had divided the students into two groups. The more advanced, higher-achieving students were called the Eagles. The lower achievers were labeled the Turtles. The first teacher had actually put these labels on the board and listed the children's names under them! The new teacher was horrified and heartbroken. "I often wonder," she said, "how many of these students will forever feel that they are turtles."

As adults, we influence even the youngest babies by responding to them and showing them what we value: "Oh, he cooed, he's so verbal!" "She follows me with her eyes, she likes me!" "Look at how she grabs my finger, what a strong kid!" We are constantly labeling children's behavior. Sometimes we do so after long and thoughtful analysis, sometimes hastily when we're mad or tired or on overload. Whatever the situation, kids listen to us and believe us.

Establish Rituals. Who hasn't sighed over those pretty greeting-card images of large extended families sharing leisurely holidays together? Yet contemporary families are often scattered geographically, so few of us have this luxury today. Sometimes it seems nearly impossible to get most family members in the same place at the same time. Nevertheless, children today need the structure and reassurance of family rituals as much as ever if they are going to be resilient.

What regular "rituals" do you practice? (They don't have to be elaborate: storytime and regular shared meals are important anchors for kids.) What others can you start? It may take a bit of ingenuity to establish new family rituals for the twenty-first-century child, but it pays benefits for a lifetime.

Encourage Independence and Responsibility. Model goal-setting behavior, and encourage your children to imitate you. What realistic goals can they set today? What are they mature enough to take responsibility for? The trading of privileges for duties is an age-old struggle between parent and child, with each trying to get the best of the deal. I suggest that you focus on the positive emotional benefits to the child of assuming the new responsibility, rather than the "payment" in privileges. (Let the child hear you describing this new maturity with pride and excitement: "Kevin has learned how to stack his blocks on the shelf at bedtime!" "Laura can vacuum the living room now!")

Be Consistently Responsive and Positive. The most important thing you can give your children is not a thing. It's yourself. There is nothing more lasting or appreciated. Life's most valuable lessons are seldom learned from formal instruction. Most often, they are passed from one generation to another during those special moments of family togetherness. Think back to such a time in your life. Aren't these memories a source of inspiration and strength? I'm sure you were unaware that anything miraculous had happened. Yet, in retrospect, we all recognize the significance of these experiences.

Several years ago I was at a national seminar for Bristol-Myers Squibb pharmaceutical sales representatives. As part of an exercise, each rep was asked to describe the greatest gift he or she had ever received. One young man stood and said, "I'll always remember a small box my father gave me one Christmas. Inside was a note that said, 'I will give you 365 hours of my total attention every year. We can use this time to do whatever you want. This is my gift to you.'" The man said that he'd forgotten most of his childhood presents, but he would always remember this one.

PROFILE
Flo Wheatley

One bitter winter morning, Flo Wheatley of Hop Bottom, Pennsylvania, took her son to Manhattan for a medical checkup. As they hurried through the cold, she noticed many homeless people huddled in doorways. One stood out from the others because he was wrapped in a bright pink hand-knit afghan.

Most of us have had similar encounters and felt helpless to do anything. No one of us alone can solve the staggering economic and social problems behind this urban tragedy. So most of us just avert our eyes.

Not Flo Wheatley. As a nurse, she knew well the lethal potential of hypothermia. She couldn't stop thinking about that man and his handmade blanket. Flo realized that she couldn't hope to save all the potential freezing victims, but she might be able to help one.

Back home that night, she took a pile of her children's castoff clothing and some old bedspreads and quickly assembled them into a simple sleeping bag. This first emergency sleeping bag was so gratefully received by a homeless person that she and her family continued to turn them out. That first year they made eight, which she and her husband, Jim, distributed themselves. Soon neighbors began to notice this unusual activity. Once they saw the potential for saving lives with recycled discards, they enthusiastically joined in. The project grew and acquired a name, My Brother's Keeper Quilt Group.

Today, Flo Wheatley is the dynamic leader behind a nationwide movement of thousands of volunteers in dozens of cities and towns. Volunteers with her grassroots project have produced and distributed more than one hundred thousand free emergency sleeping bags for the homeless population, made entirely from recycled materials that would otherwise have been discarded. As of 1996, Flo and Jim have had forty-nine thousand Ugly Quilts (as these bags are sometimes called) pass through their own garage distribution center, and thousands more are being made and given away by church groups, youth groups, and individuals around the country. The cost-free procedure that started on her kitchen table has grown into a nonprofit organization with a thirteen-member board of directors. Flo's home has become command central for the project, as she shares information and connects donors, volunteers, and distributors. Her front porch, barn, and garage have all acted as a temporary clearinghouse for local donations, and her calendar is crowded with how-to pep talks for churches and civic organizations. Flo's basic message is simple: "Start here. Start now. Everyone can do something."

Flo Wheatley has become a true leader because she has provided thousands with the inspiration, motivation, and method necessary to confront a national crisis, as well as the opportunity to find the best in themselves.

R E S I L I E N C E   B U I L D E R

Develop Your Leadership

1. Define Your Circle of Influence

- Who now looks to you as a leader? How do you demonstrate your resilience to them? Choose one of them and decide at least one way that you can help this person build his or her own resilience. Create a strategy and carry it out.
- Who are some other people you would like to look up to you as a leader? How can you demonstrate your own resilience to them?

2. Recognize Your Leadership Abilities

Complete the following examples:

- A vision I'm eager to share with others is:
- An example of my ability to stimulate achievement is:
- A time when I overcame resistance by sharing my values was:
- I helped others reinterpret change or crisis when I:
- I earn the trust of others by:
- I expanded the horizons of someone when I:
- A recent occasion when results were disappointing, but I emphasized the positive—the equality of the work or the flexibility of the workers was:
- My ability to get people working together is:

If you can't immediately come up with a strong, positive example for any point, go back and reread the appropriate section in this chapter. Then envision yourself demonstrating this skill. Seek out a situation where you can put your mental script into action.

3. Build Resilience in Others

Inspire them. Think of an idea or project that you'd like others to support. Write a vivid description of this project, first emphasizing the outcome rather than the process, then describing your vision of how those who participate will benefit and grow with the process. (Draw on all your "creative-writing" skills.)

Coach them. How do you help others to feel important? How do you try to communicate that someone is a valued contributor to the team or project? How successful are you at this? What else could you do?

Empower them. How do you encourage a sense of control in your followers? What controls are you willing and/or able to give them? What teams do you lead? What teams are you a member of? How could these teams be healthier, stronger, more productive? Is it within your power to carry this out or persuade others to do so?

Who's Leading?

I met my wife, Donna, when she hired me as keynote speaker for a lecture series at Louisiana Tech University. She had narrowed her decision down to myself and Wally "Famous" Amos—the chocolate-chip cookie entrepreneur. Lucky for me, Wally was already booked. I've never been so happy to be second choice!

Soon after we were married, Donna broke me of one of my bad habits. She is a very bright lady and, understandably, she resented my tendency to "micro-manage" everything, as she called it. I'd give directions for the most obvious things. Finally, she decided to teach me a lesson. She was dropping me off in a parking lot. As I got out of the car, I automatically began my litany of instructions.

"Donna, did you see the sign back there? It said No Exit—Spikes Will Cause Severe Tire Damage. So, whatever you do, don't drive out that way." Donna smiled sweetly, put the car in gear, and roared off right toward the forbidden exit. I let out a yell and sprinted after her, waving frantically. Just short of the spikes, she hit the brakes. When I reached the car, huffing and puffing, she rolled down the window. She was laughing so hard she could hardly catch her breath, and in a moment I was too. I learned not to doubt her eyesight and intelligence, and we both gave ourselves permission to laugh at our foibles and blind spots. In the dance of life, both partners can lead.

9

Embrace Challenges

Once I was served the most delicious piece of pineapple upside-down cake I've ever had—incredibly rich but not cloyingly sweet. Afterward I had to ask what the secret was. The answer delighted me: lemon juice! Just that little bit of tartness made the flavor all the sweeter.

Sometimes it takes the sour to reveal the unexpected sweetness amid our challenges. Without adversity, we would never develop the qualities of resourcefulness, flexibility, and perseverance that are essential to continuing success. We become strong because we've struggled, while those who flee from challenges stay soft and flabby, physically, mentally, and emotionally.

Life is not always gentle. It can hand out discouragement, disappointment, and loss. We meet life's challenges when we confront, think through, and finally master the problems before us.

And as time passes, we discover that it was from these experiences that we have gained the most insight.

Nonresilient people define "challenges" as something negative, like a fight or a major difficulty. What reasonable person would go around looking for such bad stuff to happen? Yet, although resilient people are exceptionally reasonable, they rarely shy away from a good challenge. Sometimes they even seek them out. The secret is in how they define and use challenges.

Recently I stood on the heights of Waimea on Kauai Island, Hawaii, looking down at the ocean far below. The water looked smooth as glass, calm and serene. Yet when we descended the hill and drew near the beach, I saw that the water was actually rough and choppy, with waves crashing on the rocks. What a difference between my perception from a distance and the reality of close up! It reminded me of my experiences while writing this book. Often I met people who seemed to have smooth, trouble-free lives, but as I talked to them and found out more about them, I saw that they had also faced choppy waters. I realized that no one, whatever image they present to the world, is immune from challenge.

Planning Versus Preparation

Planning and preparation seem very similar, but there is one important difference. We *plan* to meet our goals, but we *prepare* to meet our challenges.

BOUNCE HIGHER TIP

Prepare and *plan*
to achieve what you can.

Today's fast-paced, rapidly changing world makes planning alone impractical. If we can't predict the future accurately, how can we hope to plan for every conceivable eventuality? A message I constantly share with my audiences is that having a flexible plan is essential, but you'd better also be properly *prepared*.

Planning assumes that you're fairly certain what the future will bring. Sometimes you've scoped out the other players accurately, but other times you face unfamiliar opponents with unknown weapons in their arsenals.

The same is true of life. When you get up in the morning, you can't always be sure what the day will bring. My solution is to plan well and wisely, but to be prepared to cope with the unexpected. Of course you prepare in material and practical ways, keeping resources in reserve and maintaining a wide base of skills. But even more important is mental preparation.

A PREPARED ATTITUDE

1. I believe that, ultimately, I will triumph.
2. I know I can stay flexible.
3. I am hungry for new challenges, even this one.
4. I can draw strength from my past experiences.
5. I have a wealth of unique personal resources to use.
6. I am committed to self-mastery. That means I can accept the past and move forward with my life.
7. I realize that being courageous doesn't mean I'm not afraid.

Planning tends to be fairly rigid, setting a well-defined course to follow. *Preparation*, on the other hand, requires flexibility. As admirable and useful as well-designed plans are, they don't always allow for future uncertainties. But when we both plan and prepare, then negative incidents are less stressful, and we keep ourselves open to unexpected opportunities. Uncertainty may cause us to doubt our plans, but if we trust the adequacy of our preparation, we won't lose our momentum and focus.

Here's what I've learned. If you have a solid and foolproof game plan to beat your opponents, that's terrific—as long as your opponents adapt themselves to your plan. But if they don't, then you have to rely on your preparation so you can adapt yourself to the other guy's game plan. Too often we are lured into thinking that as long as we have the right plan it will keep us safe and prevent us from making mistakes. But only solid preparation will keep us truly flexible and empower us to handle the unexpected.

People sometimes tell me that they're angry, frustrated, and discouraged because their well-thought-out plan has somehow failed them. That's one of the problems with just planning but not preparing. A good plan lays out a clear set of criteria for achievement. Any deviation may be called "failure." But when you add good preparation to your planning, you're able to discover new paths to success in these deviations.

On the tennis court, they say, "Failure follows those who fail to follow through." That's why I urge people to *prepare* as well as plan by strengthening the skills and attitudes that make up their resilience. Then, when new opportunities arise (as they inevitably will), they're ready to take full advantage of them.

The Challenge of Fear

Fear is caused by circumstances. Anxiety is generated by imagination or memory. Fear is a very useful emotion. This may surprise you. Shouldn't resilience make us immune to fear? Fortunately not, because fear alerts us to a dangerous situation. The classic fight-or-flight response to fear can serve a very practical purpose. True fear helps us anticipate problems, take precautions, and strengthen our efforts. It makes us do practical things like buckling our seat belts, brushing and flossing, and installing smoke alarms.

Anxiety, on the other hand, is useless. It is not a response to any real danger, and the resilient learn to avoid it. It is invariably negative and unmotivating. Anxiety, by definition, is the anticipation of a negative event. When you are anxious, you are imagining a possible future challenge. It's easy to film our own Coming Attractions, using negative self-expectancy to predict every possible thing that could go wrong, and then presenting these catastrophes in glorious Technicolor with Dolby sound. With practice, we can turn anxiety into a permanent bad habit that paralyzes us and throttles our unique talents and abilities.

The ancients saw the dual nature of crisis. Our modern word comes from the Greek *krisis*, which means "decision," a time of choice. The Chinese ideograph for crisis combines the elements of two other characters, "moment of danger" and "opportunity." When crisis presents danger and threatens our vital resources, it can seem like an enemy, triggering the fight-or-flight reflex. But crisis may also offer an opportunity to feel challenged, to grow, and to master.

After actor Christopher Reeve was paralyzed, he said he decided to view his life as a prism. Sometimes, as he rotates it in his mind, it fails to transmit light and everything seems dark. But then he continues to turn it and suddenly he discovers brilliant new colors. When you decide to reinterpret a crisis as a challenge, you can grab its momentum and energy for yourself, riding it like a powerful wave.

What do people fear most? Let's look at five common fears.

Fear of Losing Control. "Better the devil you know than the one you don't know." We all fear that we will lose the carefully-built-up position that seems to define us. Being forced to redefine ourselves can be a terrifying prospect.

Fear of Deciding. Being asked to choose one thing over another forces us to answer the tough question, "What do I really want?" Having to commit to one thing may eliminate future options. As long as we don't choose, all possibilities are theoretically still available.

Fear of Rejection. Any time you change, you risk upsetting others. They have to redefine you and the dynamics of their relationship with you. What if they don't like the new you and prefer you the way you used to be?

Fear of Failure. If you commit to achieving something, you and others will notice if you fall short or fail. Better not to risk such exposure.

Fear of Success. If you strive mightily and change for the better, others may expect even more from you and make new demands. It's easier not to get trapped by their ever-rising expectations.

I'm sure you've noticed by now that *none* of these common "fears" actually qualifies as a real fear. All are just anxieties about possible ways we can fail. How do you separate the nagging feeling that something isn't right (often a good early-warning signal) from the discomfort that accompanies any major change?

DISCOMFORT? OR REAL DANGER?

Ask yourself:
1. What's the worst that can happen?
2. Can I live with that?
3. What's the best that can happen?
4. Can I live without that?

Then decide if your discomfort is an action-promoting fear or just an immobilizing anxiety. Can you afford to take a risk? Can you afford not to?

Celebrate the discomfort that some call fear because it means you're stepping out of your comfort zone. Sometimes you'll feel uneasy when you face a challenge, but keep your excitement and expectation high by seeing it as a new opportunity. Remove *failure* from your vocabulary, and replace it with words like *setback*, *glitch*, *temporary bump in the road*, or *learning experience*.

In a competitive environment, a risk-taking philosophy helps to break the anxiety block and develop the all-important edge to outperform your opponents. As the adage says, If you don't do something different, you'll end up where you're headed. The secret is to leverage obstacles the same way a lap swimmer uses the end of the pool. When you hit one, use it for momentum as you turn around and push off again. When you encounter a barricade or a road block, use it as a launching pad.

When the unresilient ask, "Where am I going?" they often see a future filled with possibilities for disaster. Then they feed their anxiety with nonresilient thinking and negative rehearsal, rationalizing that this worrying will keep them alert to potential danger.

You, as a resilient person, can distinguish between useless anxiety and useful preparation. When you prepare instead of worrying, you move vigorously ahead, first evaluating, then setting goals, devising strategies, and directing your energy positively. Anxiety is unessential to the process and often counterproductive. It diminishes energy and can fool people into thinking they are doing something productive, but no one has ever worried away future challenges. You can never foretell the future, but you'll always be able to influence it by doing something positive in the present.

"Stop" or "Go"? There is a technique called thought interruption that advocates shouting "Stop" or visualizing a stop sign whenever you catch yourself with anxious and worrisome thoughts. This strategy is supposed to interrupt the worry/anxiety cycle before it can gain momentum. However, it violates a principle of resilient language, which is to go toward the positive rather than emphasizing avoidance of the negative. Try this more resilient approach if you catch yourself indulging in unproductive anxieties. Instead of a stop sign, see a red light changing to green. Shout "Go!" and step on the gas, leaving your anxious thoughts behind. Put yourself in the driver's seat and take the resilient, anxiety-free road.

When you look closely at what gets you down, it's rarely the important stuff. Professional speaker Joel Weldon has an entire presentation about this that he calls "Elephants Don't Bite." What a great image. How often we withstand major adversities and then let small, pesky frustrations irritate us and affect our attitudes. We find the courage to stand up to elephants, but let mosquitoes nibble away at our resilient spirit.

Life follows the 95/5 rule. Ninety-five percent of what we worry about will never happen. And 95 percent of the time, if it does happen, the anticipation has been far worse than the reality. Moral: Don't run up molehills and come down mountains.

The Challenge of Commitment

Two weeks after the Berlin Wall fell in 1990, I was in Essen, Germany, standing before an audience of ten thousand employees of a large international manufacturer. The air was electric. Everyone knew that their world and their lives were about to undergo dramatic, unpredictable changes.

After my speech, I had several days to spend in Germany. Two directors of the company, Petre and Gabi Eichhorn, graciously offered to act as tour guides. As we visited Munich, Frankfurt, Bonn, and the Rhine Valley, we became friends and they shared with me their eagerness to have a family. After years of infertility treatment, they had decided to try to adopt a child, a process as difficult in Germany as it is in the United States. When we parted, I told Petre and Gabi that their wish for a child would be in my prayers. None of us realized how soon our prayers would be answered or in what an incredible way.

As we said good-bye, much of the world was watching with grave concern as the government of Romania crumbled and its social structures collapsed. Pictures of unstaffed orphanages and starving orphans were seen by millions on international television. Petre and Gabi, after much discussion, tried to phone Romania to find out how to adopt one of these children. When they couldn't get through on Romania's antiquated phone system, they made a decision that would change their lives forever.

Petre got in his car and drove two days to Bucharest to obtain the legal-adoption forms. When he arrived, he couldn't locate anyone in authority, so he began asking passersby in the street where he could find an orphanage. Finally, one old woman directed him to an institution about a mile away.

When Petre entered the building, he expected to be conducted to an office and handed a sheaf of forms to take back to Germany. Instead, he found room after room of children, with few adults present and no one in charge. Finally, one young woman told him that, for a certain amount of German money per child, he could take any children he wanted. Petre was stunned. He asked her to repeat her offer and she did.

Petre told me that as he looked up and down the rows of children in room after room, between three hundred and four hundred of them, he was overcome with emotion. They were all looking back at him. He wanted to take them all, but he had come for just one child. He looked in his wallet. He had only enough money for two adoption fees—two children whose lives would be transformed by his choice. What should he do? He tried over and over to call Gabi from the telephone in the street in front of the orphanage, but he couldn't get through.

Petre went back inside, and walked from crib to crib, looking into each little face. Immediately, he was drawn to an eight-week-old boy who had the most beautiful dark eyes he'd ever seen. Petre scooped up the baby and walked on. So many of the children were older. Petre realized they would be much harder to place, and he felt committed to taking one of them rather than another newborn. Just then he spotted a girl, about two and a half years old, and knew she was the second half of his instant family.

At that point in his life, Petre had no experience caring for very young children. Yet, here he was, about to be responsible for transporting these two helpless little ones more than a thousand miles by car.

He thought of Gabi, waiting at home for him and totally

unprepared for their arrival. What would she think when she saw the three of them pull into the driveway? He put the children in his car, the baby strapped into the front seat, the toddler in the back. Neither cried. He thought he could sense their relief, as if they knew their lives were about to be different.

About an hour out of Bucharest, he realized he'd need some food and diapers for them. He stopped at a small country store, but all it could sell him were a few cookies and a small amount of milk. Several hours later, he reached Yugoslavia, where he was able to buy diapers, food, and more milk. He was also able to phone Gabi. When she answered the phone, he burst into tears. Instead of application forms, he told her, he would be bringing home two children.

It had taken Petre two days to reach Bucharest, but the return trip was made in just under twenty-six hours. He drove almost nonstop, his eyes glued to the road, and he had never driven so carefully. His arrival home in their town of Leimen was a cause of celebration for their family and friends—indeed, for the whole town.

Since then, I have gotten to know both their children, Andreas and Jennifer. They have demonstrated over and over to their proud parents the enormous rewards of commitment, not only to family but to mankind. *Challenges are often blessings in disguise.*

The Challenge of Change

Few businesses are facing more dramatic changes right now than financial institutions. The People's Bank in Bridgeport, Connecticut, is facing stiff competition from megabanks. Fortunately, their CEO and president, David Carson, has a clear-eyed philosophy about institutional change that he shared with me:

> The essence of life is change. But change is disruptive, so we temper the disruption by seeking to make our systems and institutions immortal. We believe that if only these creations would stay the same, all would be calm.
>
> This is a myth—the myth of permanence.

Reality is knowing that to grow is to change. Ideas, structures, and processes are not—nor should they be—permanent. . . . The art of managing change is to successfully reshape that which is thought to be permanent.

Resiliency is essential for surviving and thriving during change. The nonresilient cling fiercely to the past because, however difficult it may have been, it has the benefit of familiarity. It's 100-percent predictable. Dislike of change usually indicates uncertainty about the future rather than admiration of the past. When unavoidable change looms, we need to boost our resilience level high enough to overcome our built-in resistance. When our resilience is strong, we can easily interpret change as an opportunity for personal growth or adventure, a potential catalyst for achievement or spiritual awakening. Then the turbulence of change becomes something outside ourselves. We may have no control over the turbulence, but we have total control over our attitude toward it.

Turbulence Beneath Our Feet

When the 1989 San Francisco–area earthquake struck, I was working with a client in Florida. Despite all my self-admonitions to stay calm, I confess that my anxiety hit the panic level. All night I struggled in vain to reach my wife, Donna, by phone. I managed to get on one of the first flights into the Bay Area. I made my way through a darkened terminal and over eerily deserted freeways, telling myself over and over that everything was going to be okay. Finally I turned into our street. The houses were standing. Never in my life have I felt so happy to pull into my own driveway and to see Donna come through the front door. Everyone in our neighborhood was alive and well.

There are so many challenges that we can plan for but never fully prepare ourselves for. This is when our stockpile of resilience kicks in to get us through. I'll always remember the images of the earthquake survivors on television.

Several residents of San Francisco's Marina district were being interviewed by a TV reporter in front of their sharply tilting apartment building when a fire marshal told them they had five minutes to get what they wanted inside. They could make one trip and bring out whatever they could carry. Then the building would be sealed off and condemned.

What would you take in the same situation? How would you go about it? It was a real study in human nature. Some rushed in like it was a Blue Light Special at Kmart, and came out dragging furniture, television sets, stereos, and armfuls of clothes, furs, and paintings. Many were distraught, furious that they couldn't have more time and make more trips.

One woman really impressed me. She went calmly into her building. When she reappeared a few minutes later, she was carrying a shoe box and a small jewelry box, and she had a beautiful smile on her face. A reporter asked her why she was smiling. "I feel so fortunate," she said. I was startled by her comment. How could she feel fortunate? Her home was gone, along with most of her possessions. The reporter echoed my question.

"Well," she replied, "in this shoe box are pictures of my children, and in this jewelry box are some rings my mother gave me. As long as I have these and my family is safe, I feel pretty lucky."

Then she laughed. "I'm sure my neighbors across the street are going to be thrilled." The reporter was astonished. "Why?" he asked. The woman waved her arm toward the top of the Golden Gate Bridge, just visible behind her building. "Look at the million-dollar view they're going to have now." The challenge of change invariably forces us to sharpen our perspective.

BOUNCE HIGHER TIP

*You'll never be rich enough
to afford pessimism.*

The Challenge of Reinventing Yourself

How do you cope when something or someone vitally important is gone forever? When your life will never be the same again, and you will never achieve your current hopes and dreams?

Just having a positive attitude is rarely enough. People might try telling you, "Stop whining and learn to live with it," or "Buck up, it's not as bad as you think," but you probably wouldn't find that very helpful either. The best thing—the *only* thing—anyone can do for you is to encourage you to reinvent your life, to draw on your resilient spirit so you create new hopes and dreams.

As you've seen in this book, the greatest opportunities can arise from the worst adversity if only you see your loss as a catalyst for growth and change. The more unfair life seems, the more you are being prepared for this breakthrough, for forging a new vision of your life.

Here are some questions you can use to chart your course in tough times.

REINVENTION QUESTIONS

Where am I coming from? *(My attitudes)*
- What can I control or change? How?
- What is beyond my control? Why?

How long have I been there? *(My self-image)*
- Which of my many resources will be the most useful?
- What are my new responsibilities?

Where am I going? *(My motivations)*
- What new hopes and dreams can I substitute for the ones I've lost?
- What new plans can I make?

You've met some people in this book who chose to reinvent themselves when their lives changed irretrievably. Businessman Lou Statzer went bankrupt but came back stronger than ever. Lisa Durham turned a violent attack into a career of advocacy for victims' rights. Each drew on entirely different strengths and experiences. Each found unique solutions in his or her own unique resilience. No one can tell you how to reinvent your life because no one else is living your life. Just know that the answers are there when you're ready to look for them.

A reinvented life can have a profound effect on others. In the turbulent days just before the American Civil War, a thirteen-year-old Illinois girl named Lizzie Johnson became a paraplegic in an accident. With the resilience of youth, she decided to concentrate on what she could do for others rather than her own limitations. Through the Abolitionist movement, she learned that it was possible to buy and free a slave for forty dollars. That was a substantial amount of money in those days, half a year's wages for many, but she resolved to earn it.

Although flat on her back and viewing most of the world through a mirror over her bed, Lizzie was still able to use her hands. She started by making a quilt that she hoped to sell for forty dollars. Fund-raising quilts were popular at the time, but no one stepped forward to buy it for that huge sum. Undismayed, she decided to concentrate on smaller, less expensive items, and began turning out bookmarks. For the next twenty-seven years, until her death, she was able to raise about one thousand dollars a year with her handiwork. When slavery came to an end, she continued to turn this money over to other charitable projects around the world.

A few years later, she gave her quilt to an Indian bishop who was in Illinois on a speaking tour. He took it with him, and at each of his stops he told the audience about Lizzie Johnson and her quilt. At the end of the story, he'd ask the audience to put their donations for overseas missions on the spread-out quilt. Through this strategy, the modest quilt eventually raised one hundred thousand dollars.

Lizzie died before the turn of the century. Years later, after World War II, Alice Johnson, Lizzie's younger sister, learned that a prominent Japanese educator was scheduled to speak in Champaign, Illinois. Takuo Matsumoto had been the principal of the Methodist Girls' School in Hiroshima before the bombing. Alice recalled that her sister had donated money for the education of a poor Japanese boy with the same name. She planned to travel to Champaign to hear him speak and see if he was the same young man her sister had helped, but at the last minute she became ill. Fortunately, someone at the presentation told Mr. Matsumoto about Alice. "You mean she was Lizzie Johnson's sister!" he cried. He was indeed the boy Lizzie had helped, and he went to see Alice Johnson that night.

The next day he took flowers to the grave of Lizzie Johnson, the shut-in who had found a way to send her simple message of love and caring around the world, making a profound difference in so many lives by reinventing her own.

BOUNCE HIGHER TIP

Bank on a backbone, not a wishbone.

PROFILE

Paul Jeffers

Paul Jeffers is a highly successful insurance agent and an extraordinary example of the power of resilience. One evening he came home from work and told his wife that he hadn't been feeling well. He went to bed early because he planned a full weekend. Saturday morning, the alarm clock rang, but Paul didn't move. His wife shook him. She began to get frightened and yelled, "Paul! Paul!"

Paul's eyes opened, but he couldn't hear her. In twelve hours, Paul Jeffers had lost his hearing.

Paul was rushed to the hospital, where numerous sophisticated medical tests were done throughout the weekend. A famous specialist was contacted, and on Sunday this doctor wrote his diagnosis on a pad of paper for Paul to read: "Paul, I'm sorry. We have done all we can. I don't believe you'll ever regain your hearing."

Think about that for a moment. How would losing your hearing affect your life? Paul Jeffers made his living by communicating with others. He managed an office and dealt with hundreds of clients throughout the United States. Such a dramatic, rapid, and unexpected change would devastate almost anyone. However, Paul understands the principles of resilience. On Monday morning, he went off to work as usual. That's right. Two days after losing his hearing, Paul was back at his desk.

How has he fared since then? Paul has not only sustained his career, but actually surpassed his previous successes. One afternoon I asked him how he had done it. I told him that I'd been talking to people all over the world about resilience, about bouncing higher despite life's difficulties. "Paul, you faced such a dramatic change in your life. What was your secret? What are your words of wisdom?"

Paul laughed. "Roger," he said, "losing my hearing gave me a tremendous opportunity to grow personally and professionally." I was stunned. Here was someone whose career depended on communicating on the phone and in person, and he was saying that losing his hearing has provided him with a wonderful opportunity.

"Before I lost my hearing," he told me, "I took listening for granted. Deafness has forced me to be an effective listener because I must read people's lips. I have to focus entirely on the person I'm talking to. Losing my hearing was one of the great experiences of my life."

By embracing the challenge of deafness, Paul has discovered a deeper form of communication with his wife, his children, his coworkers, and his customers. So many of us carry on conversations half-listening, thinking of other things and glancing around the room or staring out the window. Paul listens totally. It took deafness to make Paul the perfect listener and the ultimate communicator.

BOUNCE HIGHER TIP

*Choice, not chance,
determines your level of resilience.*

9:02 A.M.

By providence, I was again in Oklahoma City on April 19, 1996, the first anniversary of the terrorist bombing that leveled the Murrah Federal Building and caused the death of 169 people. I say "providence" because the date and location of the meeting had been chosen several years earlier by the Oklahoma Bankers' Association, long before the tragedy occurred.

At first, the organizers wondered if they should cancel the event, but then they decided that the best tribute would be to honor the resilience of the city by proceeding.

I slept fitfully in my hotel room the night before, going over in my mind what I would share with this audience. It was humbling to compare the inconveniences of my life with the overwhelming adversity that the people of Oklahoma City had faced.

At dawn, I heard the bellman sliding the morning newspaper under my door. As it emerged, I immediately recognized the photo on the front page. It was the face of Daina Bradley, the woman who had had to have her leg amputated by rescuers so they could free her from the rubble. On Daina's face was the most beautiful smile, and in her arms was her precious newborn baby boy, Alize Bruce. He was born 360 days after the explosion that killed

Daina's mother and two children. Tears welled up in my eyes. Out of so much death, life had begun its inevitable process of renewal.

A few hours later, at 9:02 A.M., I stood at the window and watched a city pause to remember. Cars were stopped on the freeway, and people had gotten out to stand beside their cars as the bells tolled. Everywhere, people were wearing purple and white memorial ribbons, purple for the adults and white for the children. All of us have drawn strength and hope from the resilient spirit of the people of Oklahoma City.

RESILIENCE BUILDER

Embrace Challenges

1. Plan and Prepare

Think of something for which you've planned carefully. How can you also *prepare* for it? What skills and attitudes should you develop?

2. Separate Real Fear (Productive) from Anxiety (Unproductive)

Jot down what makes you uneasy, distressed, anxious. Put a check next to any of them that are valid fears—situations where there are specific ways you can prepare physically and mentally to avoid consequences. Write down what you are going to do. Then cross out the others.

3. Turn Mountains into Molehills

Here's a great way to get some perspective on the worries that can fill our days. Make a list of ten current concerns. File it away and review it a month or a year from now. How many items on the list are still concerns? (You've probably forgotten most of them!)

4. Reframe Change

What about this change is a natural cycle that can be accepted and welcomed for what you will gain rather than mourned for what you will lose? What in this change presents you with new opportunities?

The Challenge of Life

If you've ever been present at the birth of a baby, you know that life itself is the ultimate challenge. Before my wife and I made the life-changing decision to become parents, we discussed the fifty-fifty possibility of having a child with limbs similar to mine. Was the decision difficult? At the beginning of this book, I shared with you my belief that the essence of my life is not very different from yours. Everyone who makes the decision to become a parent takes a certain risk. Even if you're fortunate enough to enter this world able-bodied and mentally alert, you've no guarantee that you'll live your entire life that way.

Donna and I thought about the challenge that Gabi and Petre had faced, unable to have a biological child of their own. Practicing the attitude of gratitude, we realized how fortunate we were to be able to have a child. Like all parents, our wish was for a healthy child, but before we committed ourselves, we needed to decide that we'd be happy with any outcome. Fear was useful for discovering our own commitment, but anxiety would have kept us from having a child.

When Donna was pregnant, we prepared by reading, prayer, and Lamaze classes. I remember watching a five-minute film on the birth process and thinking, "What's so difficult about that?" All you had to remember was the cleansing breath, having a focal point, and the hee-ho breathing. I was feeling extremely confident until Donna went into labor. We stopped hee-hoing by the time we reached the hospital's parking lot.

At 1:23 P.M. Alexa Marie Crawford entered our lives. When I

heard her first cry, I was overcome with joy, aware that life would never be the same again. When I saw her, I'm sure my reaction was similar to every parent's. I counted the fingers and toes. Through my tears, I shouted, "One, two, three, four, five . . ." On her tiny hands were the most beautiful fingers I had ever seen. Then Alexa wrapped her little fingers around my right thumb. It was as if to say, "Go ahead, Daddy, go ahead and count." Every finger and toe was there.

Alexa's birth weight was nine pounds seven ounces, and she was 22½ inches long. (You're probably wondering why my wife didn't write this book on resilience instead of me.) Alexa does face a slight challenge in her life. She was born with a tiny cleft on the right side of her lip. She's had two different surgeries and has a smile that brightens everyone's day.

As Alexa is growing up, we are committed to teaching her the principles of a resilient life. The most important message is that *imperfection* is a term applying only to the human shell, not to the human heart or soul. I tell Alexa every day that I'm sure glad I'm her dad.

Being challenged is our destiny; being resilient is our fulfillment.

NOTES

1. BELIEVE SUCCESS IS POSSIBLE

page 17 *Bach quote:* Richard Bach, *Illusions: The Adventures of a Reluctant Messiah* (New York: Delacorte, 1977).

page 21 *Thousands of medical studies . . . :* See, for example, *Mind and Immunity: Behavioral Immunology: An Annotated Bibliography 1976–1982* by Steven E. Locke and Mady Hornig-Rohan, Institute for the Advancement of Health, New York City, 1983, which cites 1,453 studies.

page 22 *Dorothy Fulltime:* Details confirmed with Terry Moyer, Director of Public Relations, WEWS-TV, Cleveland.

page 22 *they recover faster and better . . . :* See *Mind and Immunity*, Steven E. Locke. Also Suzanne C. Kobasa, Salvatore R. Maddi, and Stephen Kahn, University of Chicago, "Hardiness and Health: A Prospective Study," *Journal of Personality and Social Psychology*, vol. 42, no. 1 (1982), pp. 168–77.

page 23 *People in an unresilient state . . . :* For example: C. S. Dweck and B. Licht, "Learned Helplessness and Intellectual Achievement," *Human Helplessness: Theory and Applications*, ed. J. Garber and M. Seligman (New York: Academic Press, 1980).

Martin E. P. Seligman, Ph.D., *Learned Optimism: How to Change Your Mind and Your Life* (New York: Pocket Books, 1991).

page 28 *the messages you decided to send yourself . . . :* Jim Rohn discussed this concept in his book and tape program, *Ambition*, for Nightingale-Conent, 1994.

page 29 *What are your chances . . . :* Reported in *Sports Science for Tennis*, published by the U.S. Tennis Association Sports Science Department, Spring 1995 edition, p. 9.

2. FLEX YOUR HUMOR MUSCLES

page 38 *They're less able to adapt . . . :* Eugene Raudsepp (Princeton Creative Research, Inc.), "Are You Flexible Enough to Succeed?" *Manage*, Oct. 1990, pp. 6–10.

page 40 *laughing boosts the body's immune system . . . :* William F. Fry, "The biology of humor," *Humor: International Journal of Humor Research*, vol. 7, no 2 (1994), pp. 111–26. (Quote on p. 117.)

page 41 *"What pushes your buttons?"*: Daniel Goleman, *Emotional Intelligence*, (New York: Bantam, 1995).

page 43 *The role of laughter in relieving stress . . . :* CBS-TV national news, July 10, 1995, reported on the phenomenon, visiting a humor workshop conducted by the Atlanta Convention and Visitors Bureau.

page 46 *Reeve quote:* Christopher Reeve interview with Barbara Walters on *20/20*, Sept. 29, 1995. (Williams was recreating the doctor role he had played in the 1995 film *Nine Months*, which starred Hugh Grant.)

page 46 *"Had Hitler seen us laughing . . ."*: Fry, p. 115, quoting a 1980 interview with Manuel Fernandez.

page 52 Julia Sweeney, *God Said "Ha!"* (New York: Bantam, 1997).

3. BANK ON YOUR PAST

page 57 *"Oklahoma City is mighty pretty."*: Used with permission of Londontown Music, Inc. Londontown Music, Inc., 1974. "Route 66" was written in 1946 by Bobby Troup. Bing Crosby, Nat King Cole, the Andrews Sisters, and, more recently, Chuck Berry have all had hit recordings.

page 63 *Ford quote*: Wynn Davis, *The Best of Success*, (Lombard, Ill.: Great Quotations Publishing Co., 1988), p. 32.

page 67 *Durham quote*: Lisa Durham, "Assault in the Workplace: One Woman's Story of Recovery," *Good Housekeeping*, Feb. 1992, p. 118. Lisa has written many articles and a 1993 book called *The Working Wounded: Assault in the Workplace*. She's been profiled in *Good Housekeeping* and *Ladies' Home Journal*, and appeared on the *Oprah Winfrey Show* and the *Today* show. In 1991, Lisa appeared in a documentary commissioned by the National Association of District Attorneys about workplace violence. She finances her advocacy efforts by running an accounting business.

page 69 *the 1992 gold-medal winner . . . :* Janet did the 1988 Olympics 400-meter freestyle race in 4.03.85 minutes. In 1992, she swam it in 4.07.35 minutes; that is, taking 3.5 seconds longer. The 1992 gold-medal winner's time was 4.07.18, which was 3.33 seconds slower than Janet's 1988 time. Sources: *The Guinness Book of Records* and *Sports Illustrated 1994 Sports Almanac*.

page 71 *"when others around me began to lose hope . . ."*: I have traveled and worked with Barry Spanjaard on several occasions. He is the author of *Don't Fence Me In*, (Saugus, Cal.: B & B Publishing, 1981).

page 74 *"This is probably 'it.' "*: Author's interview with Lou Statzer, Nov. 7, 1995.

page 75 *"the column is really taking off."*: Author's interview with Gail Hummel Ptacek, Dec. 4, 1995.

4. STAY HUNGRY

page 88 *"Are we poor?"* I shared a speaking platform with Dan Jansen and heard him tell this story.

page 88 *Dobson quote:* James Dobson, in his *Focus on the Family* newsletter.

page 97 *B-E-S-T:* Adapted from a sermon I heard given by Rick Warren of Saddleback Church of Santa Ana, California.

page 101 *Logozzo quote: Insights and Inspiration: How Businesses Succeed,* jointly published by *Nation's Business* magazine and the U.S. Chamber of Commerce in association with The Blue Chip Enterprise Initiative 1996, pp. 50–51. The fire occurred in 1988.

5. USE ALL YOUR RESOURCES

page 107 *she had kept the baby alive . . . :* Dr. Robert Schuller was with Mother Teresa and told this story on his *Hour of Power* television program on Jan. 16, 1990.

page 110 *more than fifty different kinds . . . :* Howard Gardner, *Frames of Mind: The Theory of Multiple Intelligences* (New York: Basic Books, 1983).

page 110 *their own faults . . . :* Peter H. Ditto and Jennifer Griffin, "The Value of Uniqueness: Self-evaluation and the Perceived Prevalence of Valenced Characteristics" (Kent State University, Ohio), *Journal of Social Behavior & Personality,* vol. 8, no. 2 (June 1993), pp. 221–40. Their study queried 117 students.

One clinical tool developed to help people recognize their strengths is called the Dependable Strengths Articulation Process (DSAP). This self-evaluation asks you to list your good experiences, then select those that can be called dependable strengths. You believe in these strengths because you've verified them by the supportive experiences. One study tested 30 people who had just used DSAP during a career-exploration workshop and 33 similar people who hadn't been in the workshop. Both groups were given an *Adjective Checklist* test to determine their current self-image. Those who had just made a formal list of their good points scored much higher in self-esteem and consciousness of resources. See Jerald R. Forster, "Facilitating positive changes in self-constructions" (University of Washington, Seattle), *International Journal of Personal Construct Psychology,* vol. 4, no. 3 (July–Sept. 1991), Special Issue, pp. 281–92.

page 112 *a great story . . . :* "New Technology Helps Spot Bogus Bills, *USA Today Magazine,* December 1991, p. 10.

page 113 *colleagues suddenly started listening . . . :* Gay Hendricks and Kate Ludeman, *The Corporate Mystic: A Guidebook for Visionaries with Their Feet on the Ground* (New York: Bantam Books, 1996).

page 123 *The most successful strategy . . . :* David Strutton and James Lumpkin, University of Southwestern Louisiana, "Relationship Between Optimism and Coping Strategies in the Work Environment," *Psychological Reports*, vol. 71, no. 3, pt. 2 (December 1992), pp. 1179–86.

page 123 *what threatened their hope levels . . . :* Kaye Herth, Ph.D., R.N., School of Nursing, Northern Illinois University, DeKalb, "Hope in Older Adults in Community and Institutional Settings," *Mental Health Nursing*, vol. 14, no. 2 (April–June 1993), pp. 139–56. Sixty older adults participated in an extensive study about hope at the School of Nursing of Northern Illinois University. They ranged in age from sixty-five to one hundred, and nearly all had multiple health problems.

page 124 *Grenfell quote:* From a radio documentary on the life of Joyce Grenfell, "A Life Full of Blessings," narrated by Richard Baker on BBC-4, Nov. 16, 1989.

page 125 *Oh, God, keep me on the path . . . :* Delivered by Henry J. Kaiser at the Marble Collegiate Church in New York City on Oct. 16, 1949.

6. SEIZE RESPONSIBILITY

page 139 *Feuerstein quote:* Robin Estrin, "Mill Owner Keeps Paying Idled Workers," *San Francisco Chronicle*, Jan. 12, 1996. The fire occurred on Dec. 11, 1995.

page 152 *In-N-Out still pays more . . . :* Ellen Paris, "Where Bob Hope Buys His Burgers," *Forbes*, July 24, 1989, pp. 46–48.

page 153 *Just before Christmas . . . :* Author's conversations with Esther Snyder, president of In-N-Out Burger, 1993 and 1996, and interviews with Guy Snyder, May 1997.

7. HARNESS THE POWER OF PURPOSE

page 171 *Sanders quote:* Author's interview and correspondence with Mildred Sanders Ruggles, 1995. Harland Sanders quote from his monograph, *Thus We Builded*, 1937.

page 175 *Kriegel quote:* In addition to *If It Ain't Broke, Break It* (New York: Warner Books, 1991), Dr. Bob Kriegel is the author of *Sacred Cows Make the Best Burgers* (New York: Warner Books, 1996).

page 175 *The philosophy of* Kaizen . . . : Ken Siegman, "An American Tale of Semi-Success," *San Francisco Chronicle*, Dec. 20, 1993.

page 176 *when it came due . . . :* Jim Carrey, in a television interview with Barbara Walters, 1995.

page 187 *I would rather be ashes . . . :* Jack London's *Credo*, first published in the *San Francisco Bulletin*, Dec. 2, 1916, p. 13.

page 187 *Stabler quote:* Ross McKeon, a sportswriter for the *San Francisco Examiner*, told me this story.

8. DEVELOP YOUR INBORN LEADERSHIP

page 192 *"you can tell good leaders . . .": Personal Selling Power,* December 1995, p. 16.

page 195 *"Never forget . . .":* Sukij Yongpiyakul, telecommunications-systems administrator at the University of Maryland at College Park, spoke on May 9, 1996, at a Newport, Rhode Island, conference on telecommunications and data communications, sponsored by Lucent Technologies, formerly part of AT&T. The theme of the conference was "Navigating Technology."

page 196 *far more important . . . :* From the "St. Paul Company, Chairman Award Journal," 1997.

page 199 *It was a morale builder . . . :* Ingram Micro employees told me this story when I spoke for them on May 29, 1996.

page 200 *"Seek first to understand . . .":* Stephen R. Covey, *The 7 Habits of Highly Effective People: Restoring the Character Ethic* (New York: Simon and Schuster, 1989).

page 203 *Saturn had been rated . . . :* J. D. Power and Associates, *Customer Satisfaction Index Study* for 1992, 1993, 1994, and 1995, rated the Saturn automobile third in customer satisfaction, surpassed only by the luxury models of Lexus and Infiniti. Owners were quizzed one year after purchase. Saturn ranked sixth in "New Car Initial Quality" in 1996, and was the top-rated domestic car. The Intelichoice Award, which ranks vehicles according to overall cost of ownership, showed a continuing decrease in problems reported per one hundred cars. The 1995 Sales Satisfaction index, indicating how customers felt at the time of purchase, reported Saturn number one, ahead of Infiniti and Lexus, which were tied for second place.

page 205 *because of personal attention . . . :* Author's interviews with Bill Marriott, November 1995, at the Marriott General Managers' Meeting in Orlando, Florida, and subsequently in April 1996.

page 207 *"Half of the children . . .":* Bonnie Benard, *Fostering Resilience in Kids: Protective Factors in the Family, School, and Community,* Western Regional Center for Drug-Free Schools and Communities, Northwest Regional Educational Laboratory, Portland, Ore., August 1991. Psychologist Bonnie Benard compiled these statistics for a coalition of national organizations.

page 208 *they are not the cause . . . :* Benard, p. 4, citing William Beardslee and Donna Podorefsky, "Resilient Adolescents Whose Parents Have Serious Affective and Other Psychiatric Disorders: Importance of Self-understanding and Relationships," *American Journal of Psychiatry,* vol. 145, no. 1 (January 1988), pp. 63–69.

page 208 *A sense of purpose . . . :* Benard, p. 5.

page 208 *In the earliest years . . . :* Benard, p. 6, citing six different studies.

page 209 *They don't have to be elaborate.* Research by Steven J. Woplin, a psychiatrist at the Family Research Center at George Washington University,

240 • Notes

Washington, D.C., reported in "Family Rituals May Promote Better Emotional Adjustment," by Daniel Goleman, *The New York Times*, March 11, 1992.

9. EMBRACE CHALLENGES

page 219 *view his life as a prism:* Christopher Reeve, in an interview with Katie Couric on the *Today* show, Nov. 27, 1995.

page 229 *her simple message of love and caring . . . :* Maxine Dunnam, *The Communicator's Commentary,* (Waco, Tex: Word Book Publishers, 1982), pp. 90–91.

page 231 *It was the face of Daina Bradley . . . :* Jim Killackey, "Baby's Timing Thrills Family of Blast Victim," *The Daily Oklahoman*, April 19, 1996.

ABOUT THE AUTHOR

ROGER CRAWFORD is an internationally sought-after keynote speaker and consultant. He has delivered over three thousand presentations to major corporations, associations, and government agencies. Roger is the recipient of the CPAE, a lifetime award and the highest award for speaking excellence and professionalism bestowed by the National Speakers Association. He is also a member of the illustrious Speakers' Roundtable, made up of twenty of the most popular speakers in the world.

If you would like to receive information on other services and products offered by Roger Crawford, contact:

Crawford & Associates
5658 Oakmont Court
Discovery Bay, CA 94514
Phone: 510/634-8519
Fax: 510/634-8517
E-mail: RC Assoc@aol.com
Internet: http://www.rogercrawford.com